A Life Well Lived

Nancy Watts

Copyright © 2017 Nancy Watts

All rights reserved. No part of this book may be reproduced, stored in a retrieval system, or transmitted in any form, or by any means, electronic, mechanical, photocopying, recording or otherwise, without prior written permission of the author.

ISBN 978-0-692-18139-3

Printed in the United States of America

Dedication

This book is dedicated to my son, Timothy Lee Brown. He was a wonderful and caring person who left a great legacy, including his beautiful family: wife Betz, three beautiful daughters and four wonderful great-grandchildren. He was always there for me.

Acknowledgements

This book would not have been written without the help of two women. Tammy Koldyke came bouncing along my street one day, stopped in to introduce herself, and we talked for two hours. We bonded over our Southern roots, in spite of our age difference. When Tammy learned I was working on my life story, but needed a jump-start, she offered to transcribe my memories as I talked with her for many hours. We became very close friends.

Louise Hawker was referred to me by several other people. She came to visit, listened to my stories, and was enthusiastic about helping me create my life story. She organized and edited my memories, helped me keep going, and saw my book through to publication.

Contents

CHAPTER ONE
Early Life and Growing Up, 1

CHAPTER TWO
Bend, Oregon in the 1940's, 21

CHAPTER THREE
California, Here We Come!, 43

CHAPTER FOUR
A New Way of Life in Oatman, 55

CHAPTER FIVE
Starting Over and Marrying Glyn, 87

CHAPTER SIX
The Foster's Freeze Years, 111

CHAPTER SEVEN
Moving Around in the Retirement Years, 125

CHAPTER EIGHT
Losing Tim 2015, 163

CHAPTER NINE
Where I Stand Today, 175

Epilogue, 181

CHAPTER ONE

Early Life and Growing Up

I think my first memory was around 1933 or '34, at the age of five or six. But who knows. We look back and remember places and people but don't know how. I still remember my first address: 124 Gaines Avenue in Hot Springs, Arkansas. I remember my first best friend. Her name was Dorothy Hill. We were the only kids on our side of the street. The one thing I remember about Dorothy was that she had a daddy and I didn't have one. When we went to her house she would sit on her father's lap and talk to him. I asked my mama, whose maiden name was Emily Runyon (but she went by the name Polly), where my daddy was but I don't remember her answer. I remember Dorothy's house burned down. She died in the fire. I don't remember a funeral.

About My Father
I have to now tell the story of my father, Elmer H. Ingram. The story tells how I came to live at 124 Gaines Avenue. My father left Hot Springs when I was one year

old. I never saw him or heard from him. He was in the Army and an orderly in a veteran's hospital. He must have been well liked because, when I was born, the employees gave him a crib that I slept in till I was seven, a ten dollar gold piece and a piece of jewelry that had three gold bars that were held together by three gold chains. I still have them.

Years later, when I was grown, I learned the reason for their divorce. Since my father was military and worked in a hospital where everything had a place and everything was in its place, I am sure my mama drove him up the wall. Because with my mama, there was never a place for anything. Where it fell was where it lay. Plus, my father was endowed with a 12-inch penis and sex was very painful for her. So sex was a big problem. Between those two things in the marriage, I understand the reasoning for the divorce. I never blamed either parent for the divorce. But I never forgave my father for abandoning me.

Moving In With Grandma

When my father left, mama moved in with my grandma, whose maiden name was Ella West, at 124 Gaines. (Ella West married Robert Burton Runyon, my maternal grandfather.) Gaines Avenue was known as "nigger town" in those days. Our house was an unpainted clapboard and had two rooms. In the front room was my mama's bed, my crib and a chest of drawers. In the kitchen was a cot my grandma slept on, along with a table and chairs and a big wood stove. I don't remember a sink or cupboards. But I'm sure they were there. On the back porch was a pull chain toilet. We had wood floors and I remember my grandma scrubbing them on her knees.

Both women worked in laundry. My mama went to work at Muse Laundry. She worked there six days a week and her pay was $3. My grandma took in washing at home for other people. She never owned a washing machine. Instead, she had a big iron pot and a rub board in the backyard. She used soap that she made out of lye and ashes.

Grandma also had a big garden out back and she canned everything. She raised chickens and canned them too. I had my tonsils out when I was eight years old and Grandma didn't have any canned soup left. So, for the first time, I ate soup from a store-bought can—Campbell's Vegetarian Vegetable. To this day it is one of my favorites.

Our Only Relatives

The only relative we had was my mama's sister, Aunt Sue, and her husband, Uncle Roy. Their daughter, Benny May Odear, was from a previous marriage that Aunt Sue had. Uncle Roy worked as a painter in the Arlington Hotel. By the time they painted the last room, it was time to start over. They owned three acres out of town and had a nice house and a nice car. I barely remember playing with Benny May, as she was a lot older than me. Sometime in her teens she got pregnant and tried to give herself an abortion with a button hook that was used to button high top shoes back in those days. She bled to death. When I spent my summers at Aunt Sue's house, we would walk to the cemetery with flowers for her grave. I also had two half-brothers from a previous marriage my mama had. I only knew them by name: Edward and Kaplan. They never lived with us when I was growing up in Arkansas. They lived with their father's aunt.

Segregation Was a Way of Life

So as I said earlier, Gaines Avenue was called "nigger town." Segregation was a way of life. In my case, the whites lived on one side of the street and the blacks on the other. The whole town was divided. The blacks had their business on part of the town and the whites had theirs.

Annie Boone

The exception to the rule was Annie Boone. Annie and her husband lived on our side of the street. I don't know her husband's first name. He was just called Boone. He owned a barber shop. He would pass by our house four times a day to work and back for lunch and home at the end of the day. He was a little man, about the size of Sammy Davis Jr. And he wore a black suit, little derby hat and carried a big black umbrella. Annie, on the other hand, was the size of Mammy in *Gone with the Wind*. Annie had been the governess to the children of Huey Long, Governor of Louisiana. She raised his children. He must have really been very appreciative for her years of service. She was an amazing woman.

Happy Times at Annie Boone's

Annie lived in a large two-story house that was painted white. It was surrounded by a huge fenced yard. Inside she had a living room, dining room, kitchen and big bathroom with a big bathtub. I would go down to Annie's and she would fill the tub. And I would spend hours there. It was one of the happiest times of my youth. My mama and grandma were good friends with her, and I loved Annie dearly.

My grandma wore long cotton stockings until her death; long cotton stockings in spring, summer, winter, and fall. So of course I wore long cotton stockings. I was a sickly child. I always had colds. Annie told my Grandma to take those stockings off me and I wouldn't get all those colds. Grandma believed her and I was one happy kid, because all the other kids at school wore anklets. I was the only girl with those awful stockings.

Hard Times During the Depression

For lunch every day I would take a hearty and fattening meal of biscuits and sow belly. All the other kids had white bread, something we couldn't afford. My embarrassment ended when President Roosevelt put in the school lunch program. Of course I was signed up, but Mama said I lost two pounds the first month.

The Depression of the 1930's was one of the hardest times in our history. It was a time of survival. I don't remember my mama or my grandma ever playing with me. I think they were tired all the time. I am so proud of my parent and grandparent for what they went through during this time of survival. My mom said so many times that we didn't take one penny of welfare to help us get by. They were proud of that fact. But still, it was a terrible, terrible time.

A Reason for Laughter

I don't remember laughter in our house or having any happy times except for Annie's bathtub. I do remember though, one instance, where I saw Grandma and her neighbor laughing together. I told the story to my mama and she told me what they were laughing about. An old maid, an aunt to the people that lived up the street, had died. Grandma and her neighbor went up to help lay her out. They bathed her, dressed her and combed her hair. I can picture them coming down the hill after preparations. They held their hands away from their body, palms out in a questioning manner. They were laughing and I can't say that I ever remember my grandmother laughing so hard. My mama said the lady was a hermaphrodite and they were asking each other, "What did we just lay out up there?" I don't see the humor in it, but they sure did. I remember they had the casket in the living room and a lot of people. I looked in the door but didn't go in.

Riding the Train to a New Life in California

At that time, there were no jobs, and the men were riding the rails to California to find work. They were called hobos. My mama was dating a man named Joe Taylor. Joe's brother rode the rails and got a job building box cars for the railroad. He wrote and told Joe, "Come on out. There's work." So, Joe rode the rails to California and got a job. Six months later, he sent for my mother and, six months later, my mother sent for me. I rode the train alone for three days and nights. This was in 1938, and I was ten years old. There was a lady going to Los Angeles, and the ticket agent asked her if she would watch out for me. It was a very good thing that she did, because I ended up relying on her for food. My mother had sent money to my Aunt Sue for me to buy meals on the train. Aunt Sue kept the money and fried me a chicken to take instead. After two days, the chicken had spoiled and I had nothing to eat. The lady bought my meals for the last day. She gave me her name and address along with a bill. I gave it to my mother when I arrived, and she paid her.

A Rough Adjustment

California was a whole new world. People were working. They had nice homes and cars. We never owned a car until 1948 so we used street cars. Again, segregation was the way of life. The Mexicans lived in the southern part of the town, the working people lived in the middle, and the professionals lived in the north. They were called "The

400." My mama seemed happy and life was good. Joe was a quiet man and didn't talk much. I thought he was mad all the time.

I was what you would today call "hyper." I never walked, I ran. I couldn't sit still for a very long time. And I had diarrhea of the mouth. I wasn't aware of what this behavior was doing to Joe. I remember a time I rebelled about doing dishes. I hated doing them. But the deal was that my mama cooked and I did dishes. So one day I said I was not going to wash any more dishes. My mama said that was fine, but if I didn't wash dishes, then I didn't get to eat. I had to sit at the table while they ate. This lasted three days. On the third day I was throwing up and very sick. My mama made me eggnog. I got well and did the dishes. That was the end of that story.

Sent to the Convent

At one point, my mom started beating me with a belt. And the more she whipped me, the more hyper and rebellious I got. She decided to send me back to Arkansas to the convent. She said the nuns would straighten me out. I went back to Arkansas on the train alone again. The nuns picked me up at the train station. The convent was segregated into two sections. There were the children whose parents paid, and they lived in the big house up front. Those kids did not have to work in the laundry. Then there were the children whose parents didn't pay and they lived in the house in the back. This was where I lived. I worked the laundry half the day and went to school half a day. Hot Springs, Arkansas was famous for its bath houses. The water came out of a mountain and was very hot. People came from all over for these baths. One of the people that came was President Roosevelt. The people thought the water was medicinal. The convent had a contract to do the laundry for the bath houses. Almost all of the laundry was towels and sheets. The work was not hard and I worked the folding tables…it was a very, very hot place to work. There was a rec room, dining room, dormitory, and school room at the convent. They asked me if I'd had fractions and long division in math. I hadn't. They asked me if I'd learned about verbs, adverbs, prepositions, and adjectives. I said I hadn't. I had finished fifth grade in California but they said I had to do fifth grade again. We went to mass every morning. I will tell you one thing: you don't want to be in a convent when a nun dies. We prayed morning, noon, and night to get that nun out of purgatory.

Whipped for Wetting the Bed

I had been a bed wetter for a year before I went to the convent. Life got real hard for me because of this. Mother Divine Heart would whip me with a yardstick for wetting the bed. Or she would make me wear the wet sheet on my back while I was working in the laundry. So I smartened up and wouldn't tell her that I had wet the bed. I slept in a wet bed for a long time. One day they came to the dormitory looking for bed bugs. You know what they found in my bed. That was when I got the worst whipping of the whole year at the convent. After that, someone would come to me sometime in the middle of the night and wake me to go to the bathroom. I was never really fully awake so I never really saw who took me.

Visiting Grandma and Annie Boone

My mother had told the nuns that my grandmother was not allowed to visit me. And that's the way it was until about two weeks before I went back to California. My grandma had gone to see Miss Kaplan, who was the superintendent of the Levi Hospital. Miss Kaplan was Jewish. She came to the convent and told the nuns that my Grandma was allowed to visit and to send me to go visit her in her home. For some reason that worked. I don't know what the connection was between Miss Kaplan and my mother. But my mother named my half-brother after her; she named him Kaplan. On the first outing to my grandmother's house, we went to see Mrs. Annie Boone. She was dying of cancer. She had her bed in the dining room downstairs. When I went to her, she took me in her arms and cried, "My baby, my baby," and rocked me. I still love Annie Boone dearly.

Going Back to California

The year at the convent finally ended and I was going home to California. The day the nuns drove me to the train we passed my grandmother walking on the street. I cried, "Stop! Stop! That's my grandma!" But the nuns drove right on by. Luckily, my grandma made it in plenty of time to the train station to see me off. I loved my grandma so much. She filled the first ten years of my life with love. My mother always said she spoiled me.

The train ride back to California was old hat by now. I was twelve years old and I was going home. I had been really homesick while I was in the convent. When I got home, things were the same. Dishes to do and back to school I went. Things seem to be the same between Mom and Joe. With all my mom's faults, she still had that motherly instinct. She brought my half-brother Kaplan to California to live with us. Kaplan was three years older than me, but we got along fine. The next couple of years were good.

Joe Leaves For Three Years

Then one morning Joe got up and went to work; didn't take a comb or toothbrush and didn't come home for three years. He gave a note to his brother to drop off to my mom. My mom had a grocery bill due, and all the furniture in the house was being paid off from Montgomery Ward. Mom went to talk to them, and they said she could pay what she could. She worked hard to pay it all off in time and got caught up on the grocery bill too.

We couldn't afford our house anymore so we moved in with a long-time school friend of my mom's. They had gone to school together in Arkansas. We used their service porch as our kitchen. We had a hot plate, and we were allowed to use a small part of her fridge. We had the back bedroom to ourselves but shared the bathroom. My brother got a job with the Forest Service, so he didn't live with us anymore.

Hard Times With Mom

World War II started when we lived there. My mom got a job at the March Field Air Force Base. She worked at the base until 1953, when she retired due to health problems. We moved into a house in Colton. About that time, things got really bad between my mom and me. She blamed me for Joe leaving and for putting her in the hard time situation. The belt began again and we fought a lot. My mom was 37 years old. This was when she started saying that she was dying. She would come home from work and go to bed and sleep until 8:00 or 8:30 at night, when she would get up to cook dinner, eat, and go back to bed. I was doing the washing and ironing and most of the house work. She was dying from then on until she was 83 in 1990. Things did get better when she married her fourth husband after I had left home.

Fun With the Upshaw Family

In Colton, we lived next door to the Upshaw family. I became close friends with them. There were six kids in that family. They lived in a two bedroom house that had one bathroom. All the rooms were small except the kitchen.

In one bedroom, Mr. and Mrs. Upshaw slept in a double bed. In the same room, Leone and Gordy slept in another double bed. In the other bedroom, Jerry and Anita slept in one bed, while Beady and her baby brother, Ernie, slept in another. Beady was born in that house and was married in the living room. When she was born they told Joe Wilkins, the eight-year-old next door neighbor, that the doctor brought Beady in a little black bag. Years later, Joe said he was a great big boy before he found out the truth about where babies came from.

They were the most wonderful family. I never heard them argue or raise their voices. Mr. Upshaw and Gordy worked for the railroad. In the summertime they moved into the mountains in a campground. They would take beds, chairs, and an old carpet to set up a great camp. They went up there as soon as school was out and came home as soon as school started. Mr. Upshaw and Gordy came up to visit on the weekends though. They were poor as church mice but a very happy family. They were a big part of my life. They were actually the only stable thing in my life at that time. Beady and I were the same age. She and I became like sisters. We were close, close, close until she passed in November of 2012.

Joe Comes Home

Then came the day when Joe retuned home. One morning after he came back, I was cooking breakfast in the kitchen when he came in. I told him how sorry I was that

I had caused so much trouble between him and my mom. To my surprise he said he didn't leave because of me. He confessed, "I left because your mother lied to me." And here all the time I had been blaming myself for the trouble! I don't know if my mother knew the truth about his leaving or if they talked about it. Maybe she just had to put the blame somewhere.

Goodbye Joe, Hello Slim

I should mention that before Joe had come back, mom had met Tom "Slim" Wingfield. They had been going together for quite a while. When Joe came back, mom stopped seeing Slim. He was quite smitten with her though. In fact, he would drive past our house several times a day. As it worked out, Joe eventually left mom a second time. This time never to be heard from again. After I left home, my mom married Slim. They were married 33 years until his death. I never told my mom about my talk with Joe. What was the point? It didn't matter now.

I Run Away at 17

I was working in a sandwich shop nights and weekends. Things were really bad at home. One day Beady and I went to the mountains with her boyfriend, Russel (whom she eventually married, by the way). We got stuck in a snow storm and Russel had to buy snow chains to get us off the mountain. We got home real late and mom was waiting for me with the belt. I ran out of the house and I never went back. I quit school and got a full time job at a steakhouse. It was an original steakhouse halfway between Hollywood and Palm Springs. It was called the Derby House. We had lots of movie stars that came in: Frank Sinatra, Ava Gardner, Peter Lawford, and Donna Reed, to name just a few.

There's a Lot at Steak!

I told the owner that I had experience, which I didn't consider to be a lie. After all, I had worked in a sandwich shop and didn't think a steakhouse would be much different. That first night of working, I disrupted the whole dining room. I didn't know the difference between a T-Bone and a porterhouse or a filet mignon. I picked up everyone else's order by mistake. After the dinner rush was over, the owner came to me and said he should fire me on the spot. But he said, "You are young and light on your feet so I'm going to train you. And once you are trained, you will always be able to find a job." He was a Greek and owned the steakhouse. He was a good man but had a bad affliction: gambling. I heard he lost the restaurant in a poker game in Las Vegas after I was gone.

Leaving California For Good

While working there I rented a room in the home of a Mrs. Barnes. This lasted almost three months. However, I spent so much time at the Upshaw's that their house felt like a second home to me. My mother found out where

Nancy Watts

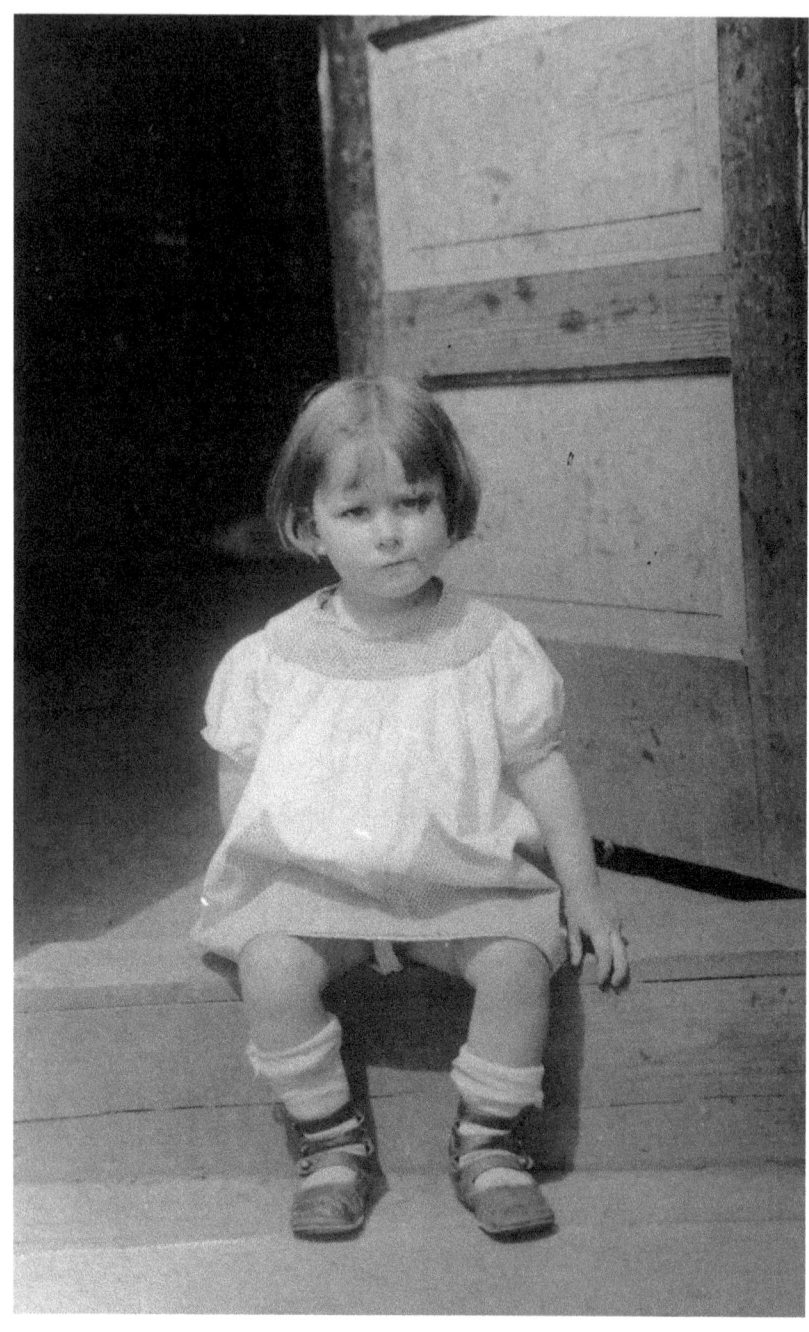

Nancy, age 2

A Life Well Lived

My Mom in her late 30's or early 40's

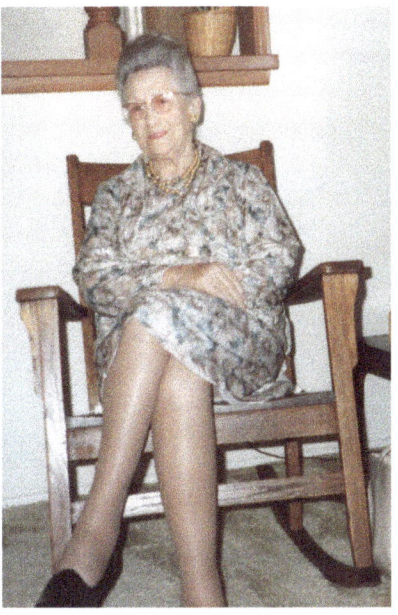

My Mom's 75th birthday

My grandmother Ella Runyon

Grandma Runyon

I was and had me arrested. At the police station, I called Beady and asked her to go get my tip money from Mrs. Barnes' house and to keep it for me. I was put in the detention home for two months waiting for my court date. The day came when I finally saw the judge. He said he thought my mom and I could work things out. So I went home, but not for long, because the belt came out again, and she took to whipping me.

I took off again, retrieved my tip money that Beady had kept for me and went over to the coastal town of Ventura, California. I knew I had to find a job, but I needed a Social Security card before I could apply for a job. I decided to change my name, because I thought that if I used my real name, they would find me and arrest me again, which meant detention and eventually back home. I had met several girls in my life with the name Nancy, and I had always liked the name so I added Nancy as my first name, and kept Jean as my middle name. I don't remember how I came by my last name. But Beady tells a story that I looked up at a billboard advertising a Packard car, and I said Packard sounds good to me.

I got my new social security card with my new name, and from that point on I was no longer Jean Ingram; my new name was Nancy Jean Packard. This ensured that my mother could no longer find me and beat me with the belt. All I remember at that time was that I was alone and had to take care of myself. Shortly after I made these changes I wrote to my friend Beady, and she said my mom still had the cops looking for me. Even with my new name I still didn't feel comfortable being in California.

I Land in Oregon

While living in Ventura, I had gotten a job and saved some money, but I still didn't feel secure there. So I got on a bus for Oregon. I picked Klamath Falls as my new home, because it was right across the border. I got a job right away. Ol' George from the Derby House was right. Once he trained me that first time in the restaurant business, I could get a waitressing job anywhere. But I really didn't like it there. So shortly after that, I moved a little further north to Bend, Oregon.

CHAPTER TWO

Bend, Oregon in the 1940's

Remember I told about segregation earlier? Well, this time, when I moved to Bend, it hit me. I was a California girl and Californians were not welcome in Oregon. This was apparent as soon as I started dating an Oregon boy.

Falling in Love with Kenneth

I had gotten a job in Bend in a mom and pop café. I rented a room in the home of a nurse. Surprisingly, I can't even remember her name. I would walk to work and pop would bring me home at ten. Kenneth Brown was a regular, but he never came during my shift of 2:00-10:00 p.m. He always came in the morning for coffee. One morning he played the punch board. That morning he was lucky and had won a prize: a big candy bar. He told pop to give it to someone for him. Preferably a good looking twenty-year-old. And pop told him he had just the girl for him.

Kenneth and his sister came in a couple nights later during my shift. And that began a big change in my life. For the first time I was in love, and, more importantly, I was loved back in return. I had not been loved since my grandma and Annie Boone. So let me tell you about the man I married.

About Kenneth Brown

Kenneth was very kind, thoughtful, and had a hell of a sense of humor. His grandparents from his mother's side came from France. His mother was only one year old when they came to America on a ship around the Big Horn.

His grandparents settled in Salem, Oregon. His grandmother learned to speak English, but his grandfather only spoke French. After the children were gone, the grandmother passed. His grandfather felt despondent living in a foreign country and not speaking the language. He went out in the barn and hung himself.

His father was Amish from Ohio. Kenneth was the youngest of four children. The oldest was Maxine, then Clifford, and Dione. His father was a plumber and did the plumbing at the post office on the corner of Wall and Franklin. He was a fabulous fly fisherman and so was Kenneth. When his father's parents passed away, the Amish farm in Ohio was sold. Then Kenneth's dad received the money from the sale and went fishing. He fished until the money was gone. He never worked a day.

Kenneth graduated from high school in Bend in 1936. Times were hard in Oregon at that time. Kenneth's sister, Maxine, and her husband, Walt, had moved in with the family. When Kenneth went to work for the City water department, he and Walt shared one pair of work shoes. Kenneth worked in those boots during the day time and Walt worked in them during the nights at the mill.

Kenneth and the Facts of Life

I will tell you a little story about Kenneth when he was growing up. It seems the little girl next door was telling and showing Kenneth the facts of life. His sister Dione caught them. She held this over Kenneth's head for months. Every time she wanted something she would say, "You better let me have it or I'll tell mom what you were doing with the little girl next door." Until one Saturday night, bath night, Dione wanted to take her bath first. And of course, it was the same ol' story of Dione wanting to get her way. Kenneth had a belly full so he told her, "Go ahead and tell!" So she told her mother the story but it ended up backfiring on her. She got spanked for "making up stories about Kenneth."

Kenneth Hangs Tough to Get a Job

They lived comfortably and Kenneth's dad had work most of the time. Jobs were in short supply for Kenneth, though, when he graduated high school in 1936. He knew the superintendent of the water department, Percy, because his sister Dione had married Percy's brother. He asked Percy for a job several times but was always put down. They were only hiring men with a family to support. One day Kenneth was downtown when the city crew was working. He was dressed up in dress pants and overcoat. He called out, "Hey Percy, how about a job?" Percy jokingly said "Yeah, go to work right now Brown!" Kenneth pulled off his overcoat, threw it in a truck, grabbed a shovel, and jumped in the ditch. Grandma Brown said Percy did everything he could to make Kenneth quit after that but Kenneth hung in there.

This was 1936 and Kenneth continued to work until he quit the city to join the Navy in June of 1941. He finished boot camp and was sent aboard the aircraft carrier, the USS Enterprise. There he spent the next four years.

Kenneth's Years on the USS Enterprise

I have to tell the story of the years Kenneth spent on the Enterprise. As I said, he joined the Navy in June 1941. He was on the Enterprise the day of Pearl Harbor. They were coming back from taking a load of planes to Wake Island. They were supposed to be in Pearl but had run into a typhoon that slowed them down. They saw the planes flying back from Pearl and heard on the radio what had happened. They waited until after dark to come into Pearl. The Japs were so interested in ships in the harbor that they missed all the fuel tanks on land. When the Enterprise came into Pearl, everything that was not important on the ship was taken off immediately, including the captain's piano. Then it was loaded up to go back out to sea.

She was called "The Big E." The Enterprise was first launched in 1936, and was one of only three prior to World

War II. She was in more major actions against the Japanese than any other ship. "The Big E" earned 20 battle stars, the most decorated ship in World War II. On three occasions, the Japanese announced that she had been sunk in battle. They ended up calling her the "Grey Ghost."

I will just tell you one of many stories that Kenneth told me about the war. They had just ended a battle and the ship was at sea. The coolest part of the ship was the fan tail. He went down there to have a cigarette. There were lots of guys down there sitting and resting. He had to step over them to get to where he wanted to sit. After sitting down he realized no one was moving or talking. Then he discovered that he was sitting amongst the dead that had been taken down to the coolest part of the ship to await burial at sea.

I was raised to be patriotic. Back in the 40's and 50's patriotism was very strong. I have always been proud of our military. I was in my teens when the war started and I remember how our country came together to fight this war. Someone once said that war is hell. What a true statement. All our military went to hell and back. I can speak for the men on "The Big E" because I married one and I heard his stories. I know firsthand the hell these men went through.

I Marry Kenneth

Kenneth Brown was accepted into the Navy as Seaman 3rd Class and came out Chief Petty Officer. The war ended August 14th, 1945 and Kenneth was one of the first to come home. His job working for the City of Bend was still his when he returned. Then I came along when he won the candy bar. We were married July 9, 1946, a little less than a year after he came home from the war. There was a housing shortage in Bend at that time. Kenneth's mother went to Portland for a family reunion and was gone two weeks so we stayed at her house.

City Gal in the Oregon Woods

At the end of two weeks Kenneth found a house. Remember I am a city gal and all the homes in California have natural gas. My new home in Bend was heated with wood and the cook stove was wood; a fire had to be built in the cook stove to heat water for a bath. I had a hell of a time keeping those fires going. Kenneth said he didn't have to bring in much wood, but he cut a big box of kindling. I would forget to continue putting wood in the stove so the fires went out.

I won't talk about all the food I burned. It was bad! I had to wait for Kenneth to come home before I started dinner. He was a good cook and had no trouble with the wood stove. I picked it up pretty fast. The house was furnished and the furniture wasn't bad. We started with nothing! I remember his sister Maxine (Max) gave us a set of dishes. They were blue glass with pictures of Shirley Temple on them. Max was the only member of the Brown family who accepted me. We were close until her death in March of 1988. We were glad to get the dishes…one less thing to buy.

Married and So In Love

Kenneth had saved some money in the nine months he had been home from the war. We used the money for the essential things…sheets, blankets, silverware. The washing machine and refrigerator were both purchased on a payment plan. We took to married life like ducks take to water. We were so happy and so in love. There was one thing that made me a little unhappy…Kenneth was ten years older than me; he was 28 and I was 18. All of his friends were older, married and with children. We didn't socialize much, so it was kind of lonely.

The wives of the City workers were very friendly, as Kenneth was well liked. We had a little club and named our group The City Kitties. We would meet once a month and bring whatever we were working on—crocheting or whatever. We talked about our projects and had refreshments.

My First Christmas Tree

I remember one of his friends was special. His name was Charlie Bishop and he was in his 60's. He worked for the city with Kenneth. Around Christmas time, Kenneth mentioned to Charlie that I had never had a Christmas tree growing up. The old house we lived in had ten foot ceilings. One day a big City truck pulled up in the yard. There was a ten foot Christmas tree in the back. We had the time of our lives decorating that tree! We made chains out of art paper, strung popcorn, made bows, and put on aluminum icicles. I had never had a Christmas tree before and I will never forget my first. It was a beautiful tree. In the spring Charlie brought me flower seeds and a tree to plant. Charlie was there when I needed a friend. That same Christmas, for a present, I stripped naked and tied a big red ribbon around me with a bow, walked into the living room, and said to Kenneth, "Merry Christmas." He said it was the nicest Christmas he had ever had. Those were good times.

Tim Is Born

In September, 1946 I got pregnant. We were so happy and so in love; there were no hard times. We had to save to pay the doctor bill and the hospital bill for Tim's birth. As I write this, I have to laugh. The doctor bill was $90 and the hospital bill was $100, and that included 10 days in the hospital. We still think of those days as the good old days!

It was Monday morning. I got up and got Kenneth off to work. I started to do the wash, separated the clothes and I had my first labor pain. I thought to myself, I better lie down and time the pains. I looked at the clock and it was 8:15 a.m. The pains came one after another, so I called Kenneth and the doctor. I told the doctor's wife I had started my labor. She said Dr. Mackey was in the hospital. I said that was great, and she said, "No, he's a patient in the hospital." I took a bath, pressed my pants and packed a suitcase.

Kenneth was on his way up to the water tanks to take

care of the chlorination and he thought he better go home, as she may be hurting worse than what she said. He turned the truck around and came home. Good thing he did, as Tim was born in the hospital at 10:35 a.m. We got to the hospital and I told the nurse that I didn't want to get in bed, I wanted to walk. She said, "Get in the bed until the Sister examines you." The nun came in and examined me and told the nurse not to let me out of bed! She is ready right now! The sister said, "If you ever have another child in the future, I am going to get a basket and meet you at the bottom of the steps, because you'll never make it up to the delivery room! You are a woman of quick labor!!"

I am sorry to say I never conceived again. We tried so many things but nothing worked. One time, I even remember carrying his sperm in my armpit to keep it warm until I got it to the lab. He was very fertile. The doctor said it had been this way since Biblical times. Some couples could have trouble conceiving and other couples could have multiple children. I didn't know about my problems with conceiving on the day I gave birth to a beautiful 8 lb. 3 oz. baby boy.

We always thought Tim was a blessing. He made our lives complete. I came home after nine days in the hospital. I had no trouble caring for Tim. It was a joy bathing and nursing him. The first night I was home, I nursed him and dressed him for bed at 10 p.m., put him in his bed and he slept until 7 a.m. Watching Tim grow, his first steps, his first tooth…when he started to walk he would crawl to the middle of the room, stand up and take off. Never held on to furniture or anything. Those were the happiest days of my life.

Entertainment is Limited

There wasn't much entertainment in Bend back in the 1940's. Winter sports were not a big thing then. People went to work, came home to a warm fire. The Tower Theatre showed movies, which changed on Sundays and Wednesday. We went to see a movie once a month. There were several bars in town: the Copper Room, the Double D, a highway tavern and the Glena Vista club. On the first of each month we had our date night. Sometimes on our date night we would go to the Glena Vista club or the Copper Room. In those days you bought your bottle of booze at the state liquor store, took it to the bar and were given a number. The waitress came to your table and you told her your number, paid 25 cents per drink to cover the overhead.

I was a teetotaler. Some people bought drinks for friends and they drank a lot. So long about 11:30 p.m. when their bottle would get low, they made a trip to "Nigger Ed's." Everyone knew "Nigger Ed." He was the only black man in Bend. He had a good business. The police knew of his bootleg business, but no one ever bothered "Nigger Ed." You didn't just go in and get a bottle; you had to sit down and visit a while, and then go back to the bar. The bar had a jukebox and dance floor.

Celebrating New Year's Eve on a Budget

I remember one time, on New Year's Eve, our friends Floyd and Ina said there was a dance at the Sons of Norway. Since the City only paid once a month on the first, and it was New Year's Eve, the 31st, we hadn't been paid yet. The cost for the dance was $5 per couple. We rolled pennies, cashed in pop bottles, and still came up $2 short. Kenneth went over to his sister Max and borrowed the $2. A fun time was had by all. We danced until midnight and brought in the New Year. Then the women started bringing out the food. Oh my gosh, so much food and so delicious. Then we danced some more and I don't remember what time we went home. We also did dances at the Ft. Rock Grange Hall and I remember we went home at 5:00 a.m. In those days people didn't use babysitters. The children slept on pallets on the floor in one end of the dance hall. How they slept through it all, who knows?

To Each His Own

At the Copper Room, a lady friend of ours played the piano. I would always request our song, "To Each His Own," which she always played automatically when she saw us walk into the bar. She called one day to tell me she had seen a little blue powder box that played the song, "To Each His Own." I called Kenneth at work and told him and he bought the box.

I don't remember whatever happened to the little box. I had it for 22 years, but like most things in life, it went by the wayside. Tim listened to the song on the box all the years growing up, and it was burned in his brain. After he was grown and in the Navy, he was sitting in a bar listening to a band. The band leader said I am going to play a song and if anyone can name that song, they get a free drink. He played, "To Each His Own." Tim yelled out, "To Each His Own," and the band leader said, "I'll be damned. I have been playing that song for 10 years and no one ever named it. Tell me the year it was popular for another free drink. Tim yelled out, "1947," and the band leader said, "Close enough, give that man his drinks."

Kenneth, the One-Man Water Department

I have to tell you about Kenneth's job. In this day and age it is hard to believe the water department in 1946 was all manual. In the summertime, the City water pressure was a one man job. At 10:00 p.m., Kenneth would drive over to a place with a hole in the ground. He would go down in the hole and manually, slowly, lower the pressure because people had stopped watering their lawns and using water for the day. At 6:00 a.m., he would go back down in the hole and gradually raise the pressure for the public to use during the day. There were water meters only for the businesses downtown. He would read these meters. The rest of the town was on an irrigation system.

In the spring, Kenneth would walk the whole town and measure irrigation. If last year you were irrigating a yard 50 × 50, and this year you decided to plant a garden and were watering 50 × 100, your water bill went up. It took him two weeks, and he did this for eight years. Every other weekend we had to stay by the phone in case there was a water problem somewhere in town. If you moved, he turned your water off and turned on the water at the new location. If you didn't pay your bill he turned your water off. The city sent him to Corvallis to Oregon State to learn to do the chlorination system. So he took care of everything outside of the office that had to do with working the water system.

I always thought he was pretty important to the City. I don't remember the amount of his pay, but I know we had hard times making ends meet. It seems like we were always broke. Kenneth would ask for a raise and the answer was always the same: "It's not in the City budget." Kenneth liked his job because he was a people person. I know there were a lot of young couples in the same boat. The men came home after the war, married and started out like us. The difference was after the war there was a building boom. They were building homes, people were buying cars and furniture. The problem was the boom never came to Bend in the 1940's.

Getting My Driver's License

At last, the day came when we bought our first car. It wasn't really much of a car – a 1940 Oldsmobile. I named her Lucille the Oldsmobile. Her upholstery was shot but she ran good. So I went down to the DMV to get my driv-

Tim, age 6 months

Tim, 3 months

Tim, age 2

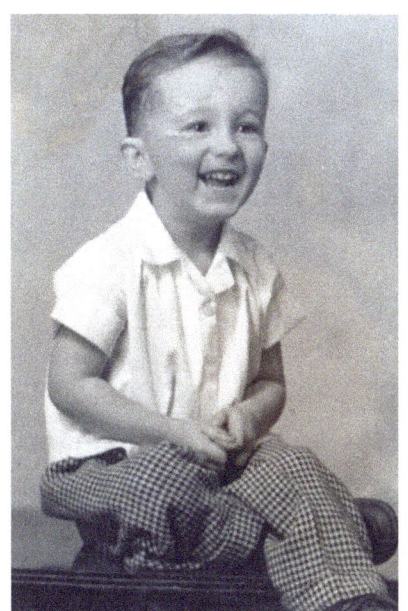

Tim, age 2

Garage house, 2017

er's license. I walked in and there were two ladies sitting at desks. They asked me how long I have lived in Bend, and I said 2 1/2 years. They asked where I lived before I came to Bend, and I said California. They asked if I had a driver's license in California, and I said no. They gave me the application papers and I sat down and completed them. When I turned them in, the woman said, "You don't have the answer on these signs that tell you what road you are on." She pointed to the signs and said, "What are these signs called?" I said, "They are road signs that tell you what road you are on." She said, "That's not the correct answer. You go and think about this." I thought, I know what she wants. The signs were for single highways, and some were for state highways. So I went back to the desk, pointed at the signs and said, "This is a federal sign and this is a state highway sign." She said, "I don't know whether we are going to be able to give you your license if you can't pass this part of the test."

At that point I got mad. And when I get mad I cry. The madder I got, the more I cried. I said, "I don't know what you want from me." She decided I could receive my license.

The gentleman who gave the driving test came over and said, "I think you better go and have a cup of coffee and calm down." I said, "I don't drink coffee, and I didn't come down here to drink coffee. I came to get my driver's license and I want you to give me the test." He reluctantly said, "OK." I went and took the test absolutely perfect. I parallel parked. I made every signal. So we go back in the office and he said, "This is a first. I have never had them go to pieces on the written test and pass the driving test with flying colors. It is always the opposite."

So I have asked hundreds of people what these signs are called. The woman at the desk said sternly, "Those are called route markers." I really believe I was put through the wringer because I was from California.

Our Garage House

In the late 1940's, couples were building garage houses. You lived in the garage house until you built your regular house. We were thinking about doing that. One Sunday we went for a ride around Bend. We drove out on NE Franklin and I fell in love with that area and wanted to live there. Kenneth said, "The City owns all the land out here," so we bought two lots from the City at the corner of Franklin and Fifth Street. We paid $35 for each lot. One evening, when we were clearing the lot to build, it was very cold and Kenneth was building terraces on the back of the lot so I could have a garden. He said, "Why don't you walk over to mom's where it's warm and I can continue to work a little longer." So I did, but I had found out that I was pregnant that day. So when I told my mother-in-law, she was furious and said, "It's bad enough you have ruined my son's life. Now you're going to bring an innocent child into this world and ruin his."

There were already two couples who had built their garage houses. They were in their mid to late 30's: Floyd and Ina Carter, and Dean and Mary Joe Hunt. Floyd and Dean had both been in WWII. Dean had met Mary Joe when stationed in South Carolina. She was like me and had never lived where there were cold winters. We all became close friends.

Kenneth and I built our garage house and did all the work ourselves. He did all the plumbing, electrical and everything. It was a big change because I cooked on an electric stove and had oil heat. NO MORE WOOD FIRES!!! He built nice cabinets and we had to watch our pennies. So for drawer pulls we used rope, which worked great. We borrowed $600 from the bank and built the entire garage house. The house turned out great and still stands—the little brown garage house in the 500 block on Franklin.

Life in the Garage House

We all remember the TV series "The Golden Girls" back in the 1980's, and one of the stars, little Sophia, who always started a story with "Picture it, Sicily, 1934…" So in my story, picture it, Bend, 1950, we are living in the little garage house with our three-year-old son, diapers, baby clothes, our clothes, etc., all hanging on wooden racks all over this small house. I pulled the washing machine out of the closet, hooked it up to the shower faucet and washed the clothes. The weather was so cold and the snow was ass deep to a very tall Indian. Ina and Floyd came over every night after supper and we played the card game Canasta.

I don't know what to call it, whether it was cabin fever, depression, or whatever it was, I had it. I came to the point that I really didn't care about anything. There was no TV in those days either. I didn't care whether the bed was made or dishes were done. I fed and clothed myself, my son and husband, just the basics and that was all. My only social life was getting together with the wives of the City workers, our little group, The City Kitties.

Thinking of Mom's Hard Life

I became very despondent and I started thinking about my mother. I realized my mother had had it pretty rough in her life. She married when she was 14 and had her first child at 15, which was very common in the South. She had her second child at 16; both were boys. They lived on a small houseboat and their only income was from fish her husband caught and sold. She finally left him, took the two boys and walked home to her mother's house. She didn't raise the two boys; their father took them and they were raised by his aunt. She got a job in Muse's Laundry and lived with her mother until she met my father. As I thought of what her life must have been like, I felt sympathy for her and missed her very much. I had made some raspberry jam in the summer, so I packaged up a jar of the jam, wrote a little note and sent it to my mother. She was glad to hear from me and responded right away.

I Run Away From Kenneth

But this didn't help my depression. I was glad that I had made peace with my mother, but my situation at home was still bad. I was so mean to Kenneth; the poor man couldn't do anything right. I yelled at him, and stayed mad at him for days. Until one night, I guess I went too far. He slapped me a couple of times across the face. I told him I was beat on all my life and I wasn't going to take it.

Since we had moved into the garage house and were able to buy a car, it was easy for me the next morning to pack up my son and drive to California to my mother's. She welcomed me with open arms and all was well. I stayed with her about a month. One day we went to San Bernardino shopping. I was tired, Tim was fussy and I was ready to go home. My mother was over in the kitchen department at the store; she was a wonderful cook. The last thing she needed was another pot or pan, so I said, "Come on, mom, let's go home." But she bought a cast iron skillet. When we got home she unwrapped the skillet and told me to pack up in the morning, take the skillet and, "Go home to your husband, and tell that son of a bitch that if he ever lays another hand on you, you will hit him upside the head with this skillet!!"

So I went home and Kenneth was so happy that we were together again. While I was unpacking I unwrapped the skillet and I told him what my mom had said. And he said, "What am I going to be doing when you're hitting me upside the head?" I said, "Probably sleeping."

Kenneth Agrees to Leave Bend

With all of my issues feeling like an outsider from Cali, the depression I felt made me want to go home to California to my family and friends. We stayed in the little brown house for several months, and slowly he came around to my way of thinking. He realized that his family had not treated me right and made life difficult for me, and how cold the winters were and how small the little brown house was. He had lived in Bend all of his life, grew up at 1015 Federal Street, and all his family and friends were there, as well as his job at the City. It was a lot for him to give up, but he did.

CHAPTER THREE

California, Here We Come!

We sold the little brown house, moved to Colton, California and rented a house across town from my mother. Things with my mother were good now. I'm 23 years old and have come a long way from that frightened teenager on the run from her. She could no longer hurt me. I had my own home and family. One thing that didn't change was her getting sick. About every three months she would take to her bed. She had given up on the dying thing since she had married again after I left home. When she would go to bed a friend, Eva, and I would go to her house and stay with her. While we were there we would clean the house, and as soon as the house was clean, she would feel fine.

Kenneth and my mother got along fine but he didn't like the idea of her taking advantage of me. He said, "You have a house to clean and Tim to take care of. There's nothing wrong with your mother." But I didn't know that for sure. He said I should take her to my doctor and find out. I had a wonderful doctor who had been at the Kaiser Clinic but decided to go into business on his own, and I followed him. I went to see him and told him the story about my mother, and that I wanted him to go over her with a fine-toothed comb. And don't leave a hair unturned. I asked my mother if she would like to see my doctor, and of course she was excited.

Two weeks later we went back to the doctor to get the results of all the tests. They came to the waiting room and called my mother back. But before she could walk back, the doctor came out to the waiting room and sat down next to us. He said, "You were right Nancy. She is a full blown hypochondriac. When she talks about her ailments she lights up like a Christmas tree. She was in very good health but had one plugged artery." Then the doctor said, "President Eisenhower had several blocked arteries and he will live another two years. She will have to have her gall bladder removed in a few years. But other than that, she is fine." Two years later President Eisenhower died, and one year after that mom had her gall bladder removed. When mom got sick after that, I told her "You'll be fine," unless of course she was running a temperature. No more babysitting mom!

This was in 1951, just before the Korean War, and there was a recession going on. So Kenneth was having a hard time finding a job. One day I was visiting one of my girlfriends, Lowanda Scott, and I was telling her about Kenneth and the job situation. She said, "Why don't you go next door and talk to Frank Parissi? He works at Kaiser

Steel." So I did, even though Kenneth had already submitted an application at Kaiser. Frank was packing his lunch, ready to leave for work. He told me to write Kenneth's name on a piece of paper, which he took. The next morning, Kaiser called Kenneth and offered him a job. It's not what you know, but who you know!

Living the Good Life

The first day Kenneth worked at Kaiser, they gave him a stick with a nail in the end and told him to pick up trash in the yard. Less than a year later he was a foreman of the yard. I went to work as a checker in a supermarket that was union. I was making $4.10/hour, and the minimum wage was around $2/hour, so we were both making good money. During this time, I remembered when I was growing up in "Nigger town," I always wanted to have more for myself. I wanted the best house on the best street, and I wanted my child to have everything I didn't have. So Kenneth and I bought the house; we had two new cars in the driveway. Tim had a new bike but wanted a Schwinn, so we bought it.

So I had reached my goal…but had a very spoiled child!

Discovering Oatman

One year we went on vacation to the Colorado River in Arizona, as we had friends who were spending the winter in a campground there. There wasn't room for me to fish in the boat with the men, so I told my friend, big-ass Myrtle (she really did have a huge ghetto ass), I wanted something to do. She told me about an old ghost town up the road. When we arrived, I fell in love with the little ghost town of Oatman. The next day I asked Kenneth not to go fishing, but to go with me to see this old ghost town, so we did. The next thing I knew Kenneth was jumping from rock to rock, sliding down hills, running around and so energized. We knew we loved the desert right then.

A Vacation Home in Oatman

The next day he gave up fishing and we went back up to Oatman. On the way to Oatman, we passed a vacant house, and we decided that fast that we wanted a vacation place in this area. We stopped and looked at the vacant house and liked it, so when we got to Oatman we asked who owned the house. We were told it was owned by the highway department. We went to Kingman to the highway department. Seven miles east of Oatman, on the way to Kingman, you go over the Sitgreaves Pass. And on top of the pass, there sat a garage house with a privy! We were like teenagers! We went on in to Kingman to the highway department, and they said the house was not for sale. On the way back we stopped at the little garage house; it was abandoned. When we returned to Oatman we asked who owned the garage house on top of the summit, and they said Joe and Georgia Brandenburg. They pointed out their house and we went and talked to them. The next thing you know, we owned that little garage house. We paid $300.

It served as our little getaway every time we had days off. We loved going to the desert. We did this for over a year, and every time we went back home we hated to leave the desert.

Discovering Tim Can't Read

On the way to the summit, three miles east of Oatman, there was another ghost town, Gold Road town. There was an old abandoned school building in Gold Road. One day we went in the school house. There were deflated basketballs and books laying around. I picked up several of the books and took them home. One night there was nothing on TV that Tim wanted to watch, so he was restless. I said, "Why don't you go get one of those books that I brought home from Gold Road and read me a story?" The book he chose was a first grade primer, copywritten in the early 1940's. I discovered that, although Tim is now in the third grade, he cannot read the first grade primer properly. I passed the book around the neighborhood and, since we had a swimming pool, I was well acquainted with the four boys who were Tim's friends in the neighborhood. I went as high as the sixth grade, and not one of the four boys could read that first grade primer properly. I'm soon on my way to the school that Tim attends. I asked for the principal and explained what was happening. Since Tim had attended that school from K-Third grade, the principal didn't know my son but would look up his record. He said, "You have nothing to worry about Mrs. Brown. Tim is one point high in math and one point low in reading, and children don't really take an interest in reading until around the fourth grade." So I left the principal's office and went to Tim's classroom. Tim had his head lying on the desk, half asleep. There were two little girls playing with toy telephones. The way the class was run, "A" group went to the front of the room and read with the teacher for 15 minutes, while "B" and "C" group played. Then the groups rotated. I stayed until the class was over and spoke with the teacher. She told me she knew it wasn't fair to the children but, "I'm retiring at the end of the school year and I don't rock the boat. But since you are the only parent that has come to my classroom, I will spend more time with Tim."

The Day That Changed Our California Lives

I was beginning to see that life in California was not what I thought it would be. I had reached my goal of the best house on the best street and all of the material possessions that you could wish for. But all of this didn't really seem to be benefitting Tim.

The day that changed our lives started like any other day. I got up at 6:30 a.m., put the clothes in the washer, started the sprinkler on the lawn and dove into my household chores. As a working mother, life had become one big rush. From early morning the rush was on. That morning, when I was ready for work, one of the cogs failed to fall into place, and the routine was disrupted. I couldn't get the car started. After several minutes of trying, I gave up and called the garage. The man assured me a mechanic would be out right away. Then I called my boss and explained that I would be late for work. I decided to go sit on the porch and wait. It was a beautiful morning, and I realized it was the first morning I had seen in a long time. I had rushed through hundreds of mornings just as glorious as this one, but I hadn't seen any of them. I tried to remember the last time I had seen a sunrise. It had been years since I had given any thought to the wonders of nature. Had I come to the point that material things were all that mattered? Was my world made of machinery, electric lights, forced air heat and air conditioning? Then I realized I had not only come to the point but also had been there for a long time. As a matter of fact, I had to go back to my childhood to remember what a simple life was like.

Remembering the Simple Life

I remembered back to those summer evenings playing kick the can, hide and seek, chasing lightning bugs, and the barefoot days of climbing trees and digging for fish worms. What a different life my son was living. Hours and hours spent watching television, hours spent in his room with his space control switch board, erector set and toy farm yard. His only outside activities were swimming and baseball. He too was living in an artificial world. Then I thought back to the last Christmas with all the manufactured toys piled high under the tree and none of them really appreciated. I thought how different my Christmas had been in the Depression days. When a stocking filled with candy and nuts and one toy was a real thrill. We never sat for hours in front of a TV set and weren't told that now we are all space men, but every day was filled with new experiences.

My thoughts were interrupted when the mechanic arrived to fix the car. It was just a matter of an automatic choke being stuck. So I was on my way to work in minutes. But all day my thoughts kept going back to my son Tim, how little he knew of life, the miracle of birth, whether it were kittens or a new born calf, and the wonders of nature he had never seen. I felt his life would not change very much. He would go to college, serve his obligations to the armed forces, marry and settle down to raise a family in the manner we were currently raising him.

Wanting More for Tim

I felt this was not enough for my son. I wanted him to know the good things of life. Things we never gave thought to in our busy modern way of living. I wanted him to know the satisfaction of a hard day's work. I wanted him to be able to do his own thinking, to be able to create and know the feeling of accomplishment. So far in his life he had been nothing but a lemming, following the pattern of modern living. I laugh at the thought of the havoc it would cause in our household if all the manufactured toys and the TV were taken away, and he was told to go out and play. I'm afraid I am one of the guilty parents that had been

Tim playing Davy Crockett   *Tim, age 9*

saying, "Children today are inconsiderate, unappreciative and just plain thoughtless." Well, my son topped the list.

But why not? Hadn't we given him all the things in life that he needed and wanted, to excess? All we asked in return was love and obedience, mow the lawn once a week, keep his room clean, and take the garbage out every morning. We as parents were even expected to pay for these services. Since I was never under the impression that one should be paid to keep his own nest clean, the allowance was OUT! Aside from the allowance, Kenneth and I performed well. We went along with the Davy Crockett coon skin hats, space patrol helmets, and the round of school, scouts and Sunday school. We accepted Tim as a normal nine-year-old boy, until that fatal morning when I started thinking how unreal and empty life was. I realized that by giving Tim the things I never had I, in turn, had robbed him of many of life's greatest pleasures.

For many evenings after that realization, Kenneth and I had long talks after Tim was in bed. How had we failed as parents? How do you develop appreciation? By giving less?

We all know it is true that the more you have the less you appreciate, but how can you give less when every child in the neighborhood has a closet full into running over with new clothes and toys? How can we take these things away from our child and say he cannot have them? Every time you turn around, new fads and gimmicks are popping up. How do we explain to a nine-year-old that we are tired of conforming? That we do not care what Jimmy Jones has or what he is doing? We want to live our lives differently.

Realizing More is Not More

There is an old saying: "When in Rome do as the Romans do." Well, in suburban USA, you have no choice but to do as others do or at once you are considered a misfit. Try not mowing your lawn for a month and you will see what I mean. Or better still, come home from work some night and have the used furniture dealer hauling away your TV set and the kid's bike. The immediate reaction in the neighborhood is they will start talking about what a fine person you were before this happened.

We knew that to make the change we wanted, we would have to change our complete environment. Now this takes a lot of thought! We must give up our jobs, both of which were high paying and secure. It meant giving up our home, which we had both worked hard to make attractive and comfortable, and leaving behind all of our family and friends. Now there are thousands of people that do this every year, but in the process they change their way of life very little. We intended to change our lives completely. We wanted to give up modern living and get back to the good old days. We wanted our son to have a life close to nature, with a few hardships thrown in to make it more valid.

Deciding to Make a Change

There are lots of places that would fill the bill when it comes to looking for a place with no modern conveniences, but we had to have one that offered employment for Kenneth and a good school for Tim. Then too, there was the question of finances. Like most Americans our age, our home had a big mortgage. We figured after selling our home and paying off all debts, we wouldn't up our small savings very much. But after taking all things into consideration, we were still determined to make the move.

At the time you are moving, you are so busy that you don't have a chance to think clearly. But when all is said and done, and you start out across the lonely desert, with all of your worldly possessions in a U-Haul trailer and roots have been cut, a little doubt creeps into your mind. Life is sure going to be different. There will be no hot bath in the morning, no time clock to punch, no more of those convenient switches to flick. But yet down deep in your heart you know this is right, and the feeling is normal. You would have to have ice water in your veins not to have apprehension about the future and all the things you're leaving behind. But your doubts soon fade and are replaced by the sense of peace and freedom that comes deep within you.

CHAPTER FOUR

A New Way of Life in Oatman

We moved into the little garage house and opened a small grocery store in Oatman, Arizona. There was work for Kenneth at Pacific Gas & Electric (PG&E) 25 miles away, doing work on their compressors. Some of my happiest days are from living in Oatman. The population was around 75 people. Oatman had been a gold camp in its boom days. The mines had closed down at the beginning of WWII. Since that time there had been no change in the town. It was like turning back time 30 years. The main street consisted of a post office, a non-operating theatre building built in 1919, a service station, a hotel that had not been in operation for years, a bar, a fire station and community hall. The post office, the gas station and the bar were all operating. There were three streetlights and one community phone, which had to be turned and cranked to get an operator, located in a phone booth on the main street. It was obvious that they never hurried, even in the case of fire. As one old timer told me, "Why hurry? It will be burned down before we get there anyway."

Learning to Love the Locals

These people were a new breed to me. Most people would say they just didn't have any ambition, but I saw them in a different light. To me, they lacked greed. It took time but I learned to love every one of them dearly. They were old miners who had lived hard lives in the gold days of Arizona. Most of them were in their late '70's or '80's. They had a wit and understanding of life that I have never seen in any other group of people. After living in the city where worldly wealth and status in the community had replaced sincerity, these people were a joy to know. I am sure my son Tim would have told you that he was wiser and richer for having known them.

The People of Oatman

I will tell you a few stories of the people of Oatman; the majority of them came from all walks of life. They ranged from a retired college professor, a retired dentist, a retired optometrist to poor hill people. The only business open was the bar, The Mission Inn. The bar was owned by Dr. Hines, the retired dentist. The bar had its regular customers who spent their days and nights there. Stan Larkey was one of them. Stan had been a butcher at the grocery store before Oatman became a ghost town. Burt Johnson had worked the mines. Burt had a patch over his right eye. Jimmy Carnes had a patch over his left eye. The first you saw when you walked in the door was Burt and Jimmy.

You would hear people talk about the two old guys with eye patches.

More Oatman Characters

Another regular pair was Don and Alice Hawks. Don was retired from Dupont. Don had a habit when a stranger would wander into town. He would start to tell these long winded stories about Oatman every time. He would make a statement and turn to Stan and say, "Ain't that right Mr. Larkey?" This went on for months. It was irritating Stan so bad that one day Stan cut loose on Don. He told Don what he thought about his stories and always saying, "Ain't that right Mr. Larkey?" Stan got so upset and yelled at Don that he strained his vocal cords, so from that day on Stan could never speak above a whisper.

Don's wife Alice would not use the bathroom, as she said it was too dirty. So she would go out behind the bar and pee. Bill and Francis Hitson lived on top of the hill behind the bar. There was a security light on the back of the bar and Bill said it was like seeing the moon come up every night when Alice bared her ass to pee.

The oldest resident was Anna Eater. She came to Oatman from the gold mining towns in Colorado. Anna would not tell anyone how old she was. She said, "I am one day older than George Washington. I was born on February 21st, and he was born on February 22nd." Anna had never married, so one day I told her that I felt sorry for her that she had never married. She patted me on the arm and said, "Don't feel sorry for me honey, I never missed a thing." Joe and Georgia Brandenburg were old residents too. Georgia used to drive a large green station wagon, and she appointed herself town security. She would drive the town streets at night keeping a watchful eye over the place; we all called her "The Green Hornet." Georgia had taught school in Kingman, and she was always proud to say she had Andy Devine in one of her classes. He was a famous western movie star from the 1930's and 1940's.

One night we were on our way to the cabin driving along in the dark when all of a sudden we saw a man lying down in the middle of the road. I told Kenneth not to stop because he was probably a dead man and that scared me. Then, suddenly, the man jumped up, grabbed ahold of his pants and blanket and ran off to the side of the road. The next day in town we told the people in the bar about this man lying in the middle of the road. They said it was just Pedro; he always sleeps in the middle of the road because the asphalt keeps him warm. He would go to the bar every night after work, drink too much, and then attempt to walk home, not making it, and choosing the road as his bed.

Pedro's wife, Frankie, was a very sweet lady who was from Oklahoma and had never slept in a bed until she married Pedro. All her life she had slept on a pallet on the floor. They had five beautiful blond, blue-eyed children. One day I saw them in the grocery store, and for some reason I was thinking of their names. It dawned on me they were named in alphabetical order: Alfreda, Bruce, Calvin, Donna, and Edwin. I said to Frankie, "Did you know your children were named in alphabetical order?" She had never noticed and then she said, "If Pedro thinks he's going to go through the alphabet, then one of these nights when I catch him pissing out the window I'll slam the window on that "thing!" There were many more stories of the residents of Oatman, but this gives you an idea of some of the characters that made up the town.

Tim Goes to School in Arizona

In the fall, it was time to register Tim for school in Kingman, Arizona. We investigated the Arizona schools and they were far ahead of the California schools. We enrolled Tim in school and, at the end of the week, the teacher sent home a note that she wanted to see me. I went to the school and she said, "He is really far behind, but I don't like to put a child back. It's not important now, but when he's 19 and hasn't graduated, it will be a problem then." She agreed to work with him there, and if I would work with him at home, we could see him through this.

Tim and all of the children from Oatman caught the school bus. It was a 30-mile one-way trip over very curvy mountain roads to Kingman where they attended school. There was an abandoned schoolhouse in Oatman that we considered should be open and used for the local children, so as to prevent their long commute back and forth to Kingman. With this goal in mind, Kenneth started talking to his co-workers about how many children they had. If a man had three or four children, Kenneth would tell him, "You can rent a real nice house up in Oatman for $200 or $300 per month." They were paying top dollar for a house in Needles, California.

So we got three families to move to Oatman. In order to open the schoolhouse, 13 students were required to attend. We had 12, so we rang in little Rita Ann (age 4) to complete the 13th child. We cleaned the school and now our big problem was finding a teacher, difficult to do in an old ghost town. There are times in life when things just go right, and this was one of those times. There was a retired professor from Long Beach College in California living in Oatman. His name was Woody Mason, and we asked him to teach our children. He was more than willing. As an adult, Tim always said Woody Mason changed his life. Tim was home from college one summer and he went into Sambo's restaurant and saw Woody and Woody's brother-in-law having lunch. So Tim took the opportunity to thank Woody and tell him what a big difference he had made in his life. Tim graduated from the eighth grade in that one-room school. He was always so glad he had that talk with Woody.

Community Hall in Oatman

Due to the fact that Kenneth attracted couples with children, there were now several young couples in town, so we decided to reopen the community hall for dances. But we needed music. Joe Brandenburg played the violin, Myra

Hardwick played the piano, and Woody played the guitar. They were all too happy to get together to play music. There was an old gentleman in his '80's that lived in Santa Barbara, California, but he owned mining claims around Oatman. He came to town once a month or so, to check on the work in the mines. He belonged to a folk dance club. He would bring his record player, and we learned to do all these folk dances to his records. He taught us which dance accompanied which song. We learned so many folk songs I can't remember them all, such as the polka and the Virginia Reel. Saturday night dances belonged to Joe, Woody and Myra.

A Horse for Tim

We decided to buy a horse for Tim. I had met this cowboy, Bill Cofer, and I asked him if he could keep his eye out for a horse for my 10-year-old son. He said they gather up horses on the Indian reservation in New Mexico and ship them to Los Angeles to the dog food plant. He added that, after several hours on the train, they have to be unloaded about halfway through the trip to be exercised and fed and watered. He said they unload them in the corral next to the railroad track and once in a while there is a pretty good horse in there. One morning, on the way into Kingman, the corral was full of horses. So I drove into Kingman and called Bill, and he came right out to the corral. He picked out this pinto paint mare. I asked for her age and he said, "She's 10 years older than God, but she'll make a fine horse for a 10-year-old's first horse." We named her Bonnie, and I never worried about Tim when he was out in the desert on the back of old Bonnie. When you have a horse you have a lot of horseshit. One day we were cleaning out the corral, and Kenneth wondered if that old man over in the valley would like to have this horseshit for his ranch. So we loaded up the bed of the pickup and drove over to Bill Glover's ranch. He was happy to get the horseshit and said nobody had ever given him anything, including horseshit.

Discovering Hidden Valley Ranch

On the way to Bill Glover's ranch we spotted this other little ranch and asked Bill who owned it. He said it's a mining claim and I own it. There had to be assessment work on it every year, so we took a look at the place. There was one big cottonwood tree, three very old fig trees, and two oleander bushes. That was all that remained of the ranch except some old barbed wire fences and outbuildings. But the most beautiful part of the ranch was a gorgeous pond of water, with a spring that fed the pond. As you know, in the desert, water is the most valuable thing you can own. We wandered around for a while and fell in love. This has to be the spot; this is it.

We got back in the truck and drove to Bill's and asked how much he wanted for the old claim. He said $500. We bought it. Bill had always called it Hidden Valley Ranch, so we kept the name.

Before Bill owned the ranch, there was an old Mexican

couple that had squatted on the land for several years. But they had abandoned the property, and it had been vacant for a long time. We had a hard time believing we had found such a beautiful place. It had everything we were looking for. The ranch was seven miles east of Oatman. When we arrived at the ranch, living took on a new meaning. Life slowed down and things like food and shelter became very important and appreciated. We learned to live with a wood stove, cold oil lamps, and no running water. The wood cook stove we bought reminded me of the days back in Bend. We spent our evenings around the wood stove in conversation and playing games. There was a new closeness between us and home took on a new meaning. I might add that the television was never missed or thought of. Tim developed a great love of nature, as we had hoped he would. He had a great love for all of the wildlife around us; he had a wonderful understanding of animals, which he had never had an opportunity to use before. Our move was really the turning point in all our lives.

Camping on the Ranch

When we moved to the ranch there was no house on it, but we still owned the little house on the summit. So we made a camp for the summer. Orley and Pat Blackburn were a couple that moved to Oatman when Kenneth was recruiting couples with children to open the Oatman school. Orley and Pat had three children.

Orley had a tarp 10 feet long and 12 feet wide. Kenneth

built a platform for a floor and put posts up and we stretched the tarp for a roof. We didn't sleep under the tarp; we slept under the stars. We were lying in bed one night and Kenneth said, "How come we never see the satellite Sputnik the Russians put up?" About that time we saw the satellite go by! We watched it every night from then on.

Camp Turns into House

That fall we decided to turn the camp into a little house. Early one morning, Pat came over and said, "Get out of that bed. Let's put some walls on this goddamn place." (Pat couldn't even say good morning without swearing). So Pat and I would go every day to another ghost town where no one lived and tear down the WPA privies and other outbuildings, which were constructed of corrugated metal. With the metal walls up, the house took shape pretty quick. We added a bedroom, put linoleum on the floor and added a couple of windows and a door. There was one problem. There was a post in the middle of the kitchen from the original camp. We had a Redwood picnic table and Kenneth built the table around the post and it worked great. We had many happy meals with friends around that table.

There was a nice pond close to where we built the house. It was fed by a spring. For water we would empty the pond, clean it out and pump the water as it came out of the spring. It was good, sweet water. We pumped the water into 55 gallon tanks and placed the tanks on an elevated platform to be gravity fed into the house. The summer showers were over because it was too cold. Now we bathed in a #3 wash tub. One night Kenneth stayed in the tub so long with his legs crossed he couldn't stand up. It was all Tim and I could do to lift him out of the tub. You are probably wondering how anyone in their right mind could be having fun enjoying this life. It's funny; all of our friends really enjoyed coming to the ranch and staying a while with us. There was so much fun and laughter.

We Get Electricity…Finally!!

I went to the electric company to apply for electricity. They do the work on the first day for free at no cost to the owner, but if it takes longer than one day to do the installation, the fee increases to $500/day. The men arrived to install the power. I had just made a batch of home brew beer. Since we had no refrigeration, I loaded the pond with bottles of home brew because the pond water was very cool. I told the crew I would appreciate it if they could get the work done in one day and to help themselves to the home brew. I left for town and, when I returned, I had power and not one bottle of home brew was left in the pond!

We were still very happy on the ranch and still had the sense of freedom. Things were happening to make life easier—propane stove for cooking instead of wood, and a refrigerator. Our little metal house was comfortable and cozy.

Building Out the Ranch

Kenneth's job was coming to an end in a couple of months, and I was working at the little grocery store in Oatman. The store wasn't making much money. When Kenneth's job ended, the foreman asked him if he wanted to stay on as a permanent employee, and the next job would be in Hinkley, CA. If you've ever seen the movie *Erin Brockovich* (with Julia Roberts), you'll understand why it was a really good thing we didn't take the PG&E job in Hinkley. He told Kenneth that if you don't want to move, I'll lay you off so you can draw unemployment, which he did. We decided to close the grocery store because we needed a lot of money to build the outbuildings and make improvements on the ranch. So I went to work at the Safeway grocery store in Kingman, and Kenneth stayed home and built all the outbuildings. Those buildings were to be the shelters for our livestock, which we hadn't even purchased yet. We needed a dairy barn, a hay barn, a chicken house, a pig pen and corrals for horses. He told me he would have to build all of those first before he could build our house. So the livestock got their homes before me! I had no idea that I would have to wait two years before I got my house!!

We bought our first milk cow from a man named Bo Harkis. We had been told not to do business with Bo Harkis because you'll be "taken," but we did anyway because we didn't have any kind of bad relationship with him, so why not. When Bo delivered the cow, we realized that none of us knew how to milk! We looked at one another and Kenneth said, "The cow has to be milked," so he grabbed a bucket and started pulling on the teats. This one cow provided all the milk necessary for dairy products for our little family. But eventually I ended up with a very small dairy, milking only three cows, and sold milk to the residents in Oatman. Kenneth and Tim became very skilled milkers.

Sometimes, pieces of the bailing wire that's around the hay mixes in with the hay and the cow accidently ingests it. This is called "the cow is wired." These pieces of wire can sometimes puncture the stomach and intestines killing the cow. Well, this is exactly what happened. So when I wrote my folks and told them our cow had died, they sent money for another cow, and we paid them back later. The second cow turned out fine, but we didn't buy it from Bo Harkis. Slim, my stepdad, asked us to come to California and go to the dairies to buy some bull calves and heifers. We bought two heifers and two bull calves. The bull calves were our first animals that we butchered on the ranch. The first bull calf we butchered was something we had never done before! We had a book that showed where the different cuts of meat were located on the carcass. He would cut a piece of meat, hold it up, and we figured out what it was. For example, he held up a seven bone roast, which I recognized right away, and this was done until we ended up with several pieces at the end of the process that we didn't recognize. If it was a thick piece, we roasted it or made stew meat. If it was thin, we fried it. Since it worked, we followed this process when butchering the pigs and chickens. Just follow the book!

Buying the Ranch…Again

Kingman was cattle country made up of generations of cattle people. Most were nice good people, but some thought if your grandfather wasn't born in Mojave County you were nothing but a goddamn Johnny come lately. It took a while to become friends with them; thank goodness they weren't all like that. There was a county fair every fall. It was run by some of the people who call you Johnny come lately, not only including me, but also lots of other people. You were guaranteed a white ribbon (that's third place). I guess due to a lot of complaints Joe Rika, county supervisor, fired the woman in charge of the fair. When he did so, all of the other women quit. I ran into Joe one day downtown and I said, "Hey Joe, you cut off one limb and all the deadwood fell to the ground!" Joe had a hearty laugh. "I guess that's right Nancy."

We had lived on the ranch about two years. One day I was delivering milk to an old man named Ed Edgerton. He owned Ed's Camp. He sold a few groceries and had a few campsites. Ed told me that the land we were living on is not government land, it is private land. He told me the name of the land company that owned it. That night I told Kenneth what Ed had told me. The company was in

Phoenix. Needless to say, three days later we were on our way to Phoenix.

It turned out that the company Ed had told me about did not own the land, it was owned by John H. Page Company. It was run by two old gentlemen in their 70's. They listened to our story and said they would come see where we lived and what we had done to the land. They drove the 250 miles from Phoenix and were so impressed by our way of life and how we had built the ranch, they sold us 10 acres at $25/acre. We were now owners of Hidden Valley Ranch.

Tim Buys His First Gun

One day, when Tim was 12 years old, he went to his dad and asked for money to buy a gun. His dad told him, "If you want that gun, you had better figure out a way to pay for it, because Santa Claus just died. There's no freebies in life." My mother had just given Tim a dozen pullets (chickens ready to lay). So Tim went into the egg business. Unbeknownst to Kenneth or me, Tim earned the money from selling eggs and bought a gun from Sears and Roebuck! It was a .22 caliber rifle. When the gun came to the post office it must have been marked "Firearm," because the post mistress, Lou Bean, sent word to Kenneth. She said, "I have a gun down here for Tim Brown, but I can't give this gun to Tim because he's only 12-years-old, a minor." So Kenneth took the gun and gave it to Tim. That gun remained in his gun cabinet for the rest of his life.

Tim thought the chicken business was pretty good pay,

so back to the catalogue. He ordered 25 baby chicks from Sears and Roebuck. He was religious with his care of the chicks. He built a cage for the chicks; it was on a slight slope. One day Tim and I went to Needles to buy feed for the animals and groceries and, while we were gone, one of those famous desert thunderstorms came over the ranch. When we arrived home, all of his baby chicks had drowned, so I told Tim, "Go unload the truck, I'll take care of this." I picked up one of the baby chicks and it quivered, and another one and it quivered, so I yelled at Tim to build a fire in the stove. I took pots and pans and even a dishpan and lined them with wash rags and towels and placed all the baby chicks on the oven door and let the fire go out, placing the pans on the stove. And Tim was back in the egg business. So he bought a scope for his gun with his egg money and saved the rest of his money. In a short amount of time, he became a fine marksman and hunted all of his life.

Transwestern Gas Company Affects our Life

The day I learned about Transwestern Gas Company, little did I know how it would affect my life. I was home alone and a man walked in from the desert. He worked for Transwestern and was checking a route for the pipeline. He said the fly rod on his truck had broken and asked if he could use our phone. We did not have a phone, but I would take him to one. We got in the old WWII jeep and, since the battery was dead and the brakes were gone, I coasted down the hill. The jeep started, and I downshifted so we were going slow down this steep hill. The man must have been very scared, because he sat sideways with his feet pointing out, ready to jump in case the jeep got away from me! I dropped him off at a neighbor's house until someone from his company came to pick him up!

A couple of weeks later a red jeep drove up in the yard. He said he was with the pipeline and was surveying for the line. I wasn't too happy about the plans for the gas line to go through our property. We had an old goose, Old Dan, who was a free-ranging goose. I saw Old Dan sneaking up on the man and I never said a word. Old Dan found his mark and took a bite. He didn't hurt the man too bad, but scared the hell out of him!! This was not the first or last time that Old Dan had his way with intruders.

When the guy drove out to the main road, he passed Tim walking home from school. Tim came in the house and asked who was in the jeep. I told him it was a surveyor from the gas company. Tim was around 12 years of age by this time, and he was concerned they would put a big deep scar in the valley. But I told him there not much we could do about it. Tim started crying and it took quite a while for me to calm him down. He cried and cried, "They're going to ruin our valley." I told him one of Bill Glover's nanny goats had twins that day and we should go see them. I will never forget that day and how upset Tim was. I knew then how much he loved our home.

So the building of the pipeline began. We had planted

an orchard of almond trees and Kenneth had put in a big tank to store water for the trees. We had gravity flow to the tank from the spring, and installed a turn valve to shut off the flow when the tank was full. One morning Kenneth went outside and the pond was empty. He yelled at Tim for not turning the valve off to the tank, but that was not the problem. The blasting for the pipeline had cracked the bottom of the pond and the water no longer came up into the pond. Kenneth walked down the pipeline and told the boss what had happened. The boss said he wasn't surprised, as he was afraid that would happen. Transwestern brought in a drilling rig and they drilled a well 32 feet deep; there was lots of water. They installed a pressure pump and we had a well and a good water system. The boss said since we had been so nice they were going to give us a pump house.

The natural gas came from the Four Corners area of the Southwest. The gas was metered as it went to California. I think two of the main customers were PG&E and Edison. Kenneth got a job at Transwestern Gas as a night watchman at the metering station. As I have said before about Kenneth, how he worked his way up in the Navy and Kaiser Steel, the same thing happened again. He went from night watchman to being in charge of the metering station and stayed with the company until he passed away.

4-H Comes to Kingman

I had become good friends with the couple who owned the feed store in Kingman, Jeanie and Bob Tarr. They had four children. Jeanie and I talked about getting a 4-H club started. We talked to the county agent, Jim McDonald, and he said there wasn't enough agriculture to warrant a 4-H club in the county. We went over his head and contacted a lot of people and the interest was amazing, so the club was started. The ranchers were so interested in the idea that they donated a calf to each child in the club; there were only about five kids in the club. Tim's calf was donated by Mr. Getts, who was on the Board of Directors for the Santa Fe Railroad. His wife's father was Mr. Wrigley of Wrigley Chewing Gum. Tim worked hard with his calf. Every evening he would take his calf out of the pen and train him to stand in the required stance for showing. Tim took Reserve Champion for his calf, which is second place. He took first place in showmanship, which he did the entire time he was in 4-H. It was arranged that the winner would give the rancher who had donated the calf the ribbon the calf had received. Since Mr. Getts was such an important man, we were a little concerned. We told Tim to be on his best behavior and to remember to say "please" and "thank you." He came home and said he didn't know what all the fuss was about. "Mr. Getts was as ordinary as my dad!"

Tim Enters High School and Gets Sick

The day came when Tim was entering high school. Leaving his one room comfortable school to go into Kingman to the high school was a big change for him. The first day of school, Tim said he didn't feel so good. I told him, "You have to go sooner or later; if not today, then tomorrow." He said he really didn't feel good so I said he could stay home. He laid around all day and said he was sick. Kenneth worked the graveyard shift and, since we only had one car, he was gone to work.

At 1:00 a.m., Tim woke me up and told me he needed to go to the doctor because he was really hurting. I believed him. I had to walk over to Bill Glover's ranch through the cactus and rocks, hoping I didn't step on a rattlesnake, and tried to wake Bill to borrow Bill's truck. I finally got Bill awake because he was truly a sound sleeper. I asked for his truck because Tim was sick and needed taking to the hospital. Bill said he had some grapes in the truck, and they needed to be removed before I could take the truck. The grapes were in a lug box and were very heavy. I carried the grapes up to the house and asked Bill where I should put them. He said on top of the refrigerator so the chickens can't get them. So to this day, I don't know how I did it, but I put that heavy lug on top of that fridge.

I took Tim to the hospital and the nurse called Dr. Arnold. Time went by and Dr. Arnold didn't show. The nurse said he probably went back to sleep, and I told her Dr. Arnold would not go back to sleep with Tim hurting. Soon Dr. Arnold showed up and asked if I thought he went back to sleep. I said no, but he said that he did. At 3:30 a.m., the doctor took out Tim's appendix; it was about to burst. Since in those days you stayed in the hospital for ten days after surgery, Tim entered school a little late.

The county fair opened the day Tim came home from the hospital, so guess who groomed the calf—momma with Tim's advice! This year he took Grand Champion; that ended his time in 4-H. Tim had always said he wanted to be a veterinarian. I told him since he was only 13 so he had no idea what he was going to be. But that he should take all the math and science classes that high school has to offer in order to prepare for the future.

We Build the New House on the Ranch

During Tim's first year in high school, we started preparing for our new house to be delivered. It was a modular home that was assembled in California, disassembled for transport on a truck to our ranch, and reassembled onsite. It was approximately 1,000 square feet, with two bedrooms and one bath, with a large screened-in porch across the back and a large porch across the front. It's still there and still the same, with Lois Cummiskey, the third and current owner, living in it.

When we finally moved into the new house, at long last we got a telephone. Of course it was a party line and our ring was 2-long and 1-short. It was very interesting to be talking on the phone and you could hear Mrs. Snell's parakeet saying, "Charlie is a dirty bird." Mrs. Scott had a grandfather clock, and you could hear the bong, bong, bong from that clock. You wouldn't want to say anything during your calls that you wouldn't put on a loud speaker, because everybody listened in on everybody else's calls.

Don Dedera and the Newspaper

After all these months I received a phone call from a reporter from the *Arizona Republic* newspaper. His name was Don Dedera. It seems that one of the old gentlemen had contacted him and told him about the meeting with us and they thought there was a story there. Don agreed with them and came to the ranch. This is when Tim became the "The Harvest of Hidden Valley," the title of the article. Don's story was about the same as my story of leaving the modern world. He sent a photographer to the ranch and also took pictures in Kingman of Tim and his teachers at high school and the vet that Tim worked for. The story was in the Sunday edition in a section called the *"Days and Ways of Arizona."* The story came out on May 2, 1965. I've included a picture of the cover of the article in this book. Don came to the ranch three times. He was a very likable guy. We enjoyed him so much and had long talks.

Kenneth's Temper Gets Worse

Tim graduated from high school at age 16. That summer he worked in the office of the local veterinarian. After his first day on the job, the vet didn't think Tim was ever going to make it. Tim's job was to clean out all the animal pens and, by the end of the day, he didn't smell very good. At quitting time, he would walk up to the Transwestern office and wait in the truck for his dad. His dad would come in with the crew, go in an air conditioned bar and drink. Tim was sitting in the hot truck sometimes for up to an hour-

and-a-half waiting on his dad. Tim decided he had had enough, so he started up the truck, drove home and left his dad in the bar.

When Kenneth found out he had been abandoned, his temper got the best of him. One of the crew, Don Ward, took him home. When he came in the house he headed for Tim. At this time, Kenneth had never laid a hand on Tim his entire life, but now he was going to beat the hell out of that kid! So Tim told Don to hold Kenneth because Tim didn't want to hit his dad and hurt him. Tim took off out the door, Don went back to Kingman and I tried to calm Kenneth down. Kenneth had a fiery temper, but along with that temper he had the ability to forget. You would ask him a half hour after his temper fit what he was so mad about, and he would say he didn't know, some damn thing! He rarely remembered what he was mad about because it wasn't important.

About 11:00 p.m. that night, Tim came in out of the desert. I had saved his dinner, so I fed him and we went to bed. The next morning we got up and it was as if nothing had ever happened. Tim and Kenneth got in the truck and drove to Kingman and not a word was said about the events of the night before. At this point, I began to realize his drinking was beginning to become a problem. He was hanging out with his buddies more often. Sometimes on Saturday nights I would go out with him and we would meet his buddies at the bars. At the end of the night I would drive him home.

Oatman school students

Oatman school

Interior of Oatman house

Nancy saves kerosene lamp that was reading light for five years.

Our first camp before it became a house.

Our new house at the ranch

Tim and Bonnie

Tim and his grand champion steer

Bonnie and the calf who followed her around. Bonnie's swishing tail kept the flies off the calf.

The cover of the magazine that featured an article about us.

Tim and Kit when Tim was home from college.

Tim and his dogs stride past our first home in Hidden Valley. New home is in background.

Tim's graduation from high school.

Kit waiting for me to come home.

Sign on side of our store when we bought it.

Kit grooming Ballot.

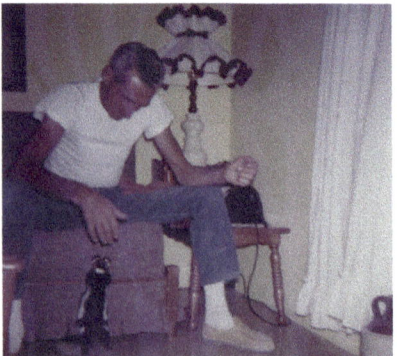

Kenneth and our pet skunk Air Wick.

Tim Leaves for College

Tim turned 17 that summer. Summer had gone fast, and it was time for him to leave for college. He and two friends left in one of the friend's old car. They had high expectations. Tim wanted to be a veterinarian, one of the kids wanted to be an architect and John wanted to be a doctor. John's parents owned a Whiting Brothers Service Station. About three months into the school year, John's father died and, since he had five siblings at home, he had to quit school and go home to take care of the family. The other kid who wanted to be an architect, I don't remember his name, found that it was not going to work out, so he changed his major to forestry. Then he realized with a degree in forestry that he would end up with a desk job, and that's not what he wanted. He preferred to be in the woods, so he quit school. And Tim was in the top ten that were chosen for veterinarian school, but he didn't get chosen. So many dreams and so many disappointments. When Tim left, I cried for three days. I told myself, "You don't turn loose of the apron strings; you take the apron off and hang it behind the door." I knew he would never be back. First would be college, then the service (the Vietnam war was on), then marriage, and he would be busy with his own family. And it turns out that's exactly what happened.

I Leave the Ranch

Kenneth's drinking was getting bad before Tim left for college, but after Tim left things really got bad. Kenneth had a rule that we always went to bed at the same time. One night I wanted to go to bed early and Kenneth said, "It is not important that the house be spotless all the time. Why don't you take a nap in the afternoon?" So a couple of days later I decided to take a nap. That evening, when Kenneth said, "Let's go to bed." I said, "I'm not really tired." He said, "Hell you're not tired. You've been laying on your dead ass on the couch all day." This is just one example of how bad things had become between us.

I had planned to leave Kenneth when Tim left for college but it was just too hard. That meant giving up the ranch and giving up everything I loved. I just couldn't do it. Tim came home for the summer between freshman and sophomore years. Three days after Tim left for his sophomore year, I left Kenneth. One of the hardest things I've ever done in my life was to leave that ranch and everything I loved.

The Pets I Left Behind

Leaving the ranch meant leaving all of my friends and, most of all, leaving my two pets I loved so much. When Tim was young, we had bought a boxer dog. We named her Sis. Sis passed away, and we had no dogs for a while.

Ballot Votes For Our Family

One day I went to Oatman to vote. I voted for Eisenhower. There was a beautiful boxer dog there. Since Oatman was so small, you knew every dog in town, and when that dog was going to have pups. I asked, "Where did this dog come from?" They said someone dropped him off. I asked, "Can I have him?" Dorothy Phillips said, "Take him. He's eating me out of house and home." I thought, "What can I name him?" Since I had come to vote, I would name him Ballot. After I voted, I took Ballot and went to Kingman to pick up Tim. Boxers are very expensive dogs. When Tim saw Ballot he asked, "Where did you steal him?" Ballot became my dog and I loved him so much.

Kit the Fox

One time the Walt Disney Company came to our ranch to make a movie for the TV show *The Wonderful World of Color*. They were there for about six months. At that time we had a pet skunk named Air Wick. We had him for several years, but he got sick and died. I was feeling so sad about losing him. The director of the movie said, "I will give you another little animal to replace him." He gave me a wonderful kit fox, and we named her Kit. We became so close. I would say to her, "Give me some love," and she would put her cheek to my cheek. She had the run of the house, but slept on the screened-in back porch. The washing machine sat next to the back door. And the door had a window. When I got up each morning, Kit was sitting on the washing machine, looking in the window waiting for her breakfast.

Tim told me later that his dad propped open the door of the screen porch the night I left. The next morning, Kit was sitting on the washing machine waiting for her breakfast. She soon started to leave the ranch for short periods of time. His dad said he would be sitting at night reading and he would hear a scratch on the door. It would be Kit. She would come in and stay a while with him. Eventually, she didn't come any more. Leaving these animals was so hard to bear.

Back at My Mom's House

My folks had been down to visit about a month before I left. When my mom went home, she said that she sat down in her living room and cried and cried. She said, "He's killing her, the same as if he'd put a gun to her head." When I walked in the door at my mom's house she said, "Thank God." I weighed 80 pounds.

CHAPTER FIVE

Starting Over and Marrying Glyn

Working at Stater Brothers

I started looking for a job and I wanted to get back into work at a supermarket. But in the meantime, I took a job at the liquor store for spending money and to pay for my cigarettes. There was a supermarket chain called Stater Brothers. Their main office was in the town where my mother lived. I put in an application and was called to take the test. There were seven of us taking the test that morning and they were all in their mid-twenties. I almost walked out because I was 37. What chance do I have against such young people that haven't been out of school very long? But I stayed and took the test. They said when you first go to work at Stater Brothers you don't get a full 40-hour week; you substitute whenever you're needed.

The next morning they called and said they had a full-time 40-hour position available, but it was in another town

50 miles away. I said I would have to think about it and would call them back. So I decided to take the job and called them the next morning to accept it. I drove the distance for about a week and determined it was way too far to drive every day. My mother did not want me to move, so when I asked her for some things to set up housekeeping, she said, "NO, I don't want you to move." So I went over to my best loved friend, Beady (Eloise), and told her what I needed. She said, "Let's see what we can gather up." So she set me up in housekeeping.

A New Life: Apartment and Job

I rented an apartment about three blocks from the store I'd be working in. The morning I walked in to Stater Brothers I knew no one. New job, new people, new environment, etc. I think I kind of felt like a jackrabbit that I used to see so much of on the ranch. If you picked up that jackrabbit and put it in a city, an unfamiliar environment, imagine what it would think and how it would feel. But the 32 employees at Stater Brothers became my family. We were all very close and supported each other as the best of friends. From top management to the lowest employee, there was no difference in status, as we all related to each other on the same level. We usually met at the Rebel Room, the little bar across the street, and had such a good time together. I didn't drink, but many of the employees drank and got drunk, and we all laughed it up.

Having a Son in College

Still, this was a lonely time in my life. I had not lived alone since I was 18 years old. I missed Tim so much. We talked on the phone a lot. He came at Christmas time and Easter and worked all summer for the Transwestern pipeline. His dad got him the job at Transwestern. He worked every summer while in college and saved his money all summer for school in the fall. When he graduated from high school, his dad opened a checking account, put $500 in the account and gave Tim a gold watch. He told him not to ever ask him for anything else. Kind of like when he told Tim, when he was 10 years old, that Santa Claus has just died. There's no freebies in life.

In Tim's junior year, he ran out of money the last three weeks of school. He called me and said he hadn't had anything to eat for 24 hours. I asked him, "For God sakes, why did you wait 24 hours? I will send you $50. And tomorrow is payday, and I will send you another $50." I went down to Western Union and sent him the money. He called later and said his income tax refund check that he was depending on had come in, and not to send any more money.

Earlier, Tim needed dental work done and called his dad for the money. His dad said for Tim to get the dental work done and then he would reimburse him. So Tim did as his dad said, but when it came time for the reimbursement, his dad didn't come through on his promise. The $100 that I sent Tim was the total amount he received from me and his dad for four years of college. It was a testament to his character that he completely supported himself and paid for his college education, including all expenses, by working hard each summer and part-time during the school year, and graduated debt free! He graduated with a B.S. in Chemistry from University of Arizona in Tucson.

Tim Joins the Navy

One evening the phone rang and I knew it was Tim because it was a couple days after graduation. He said, "Hi mom, I am now a member of the U.S. Navy." I said "W H A T ? ? ? How did this all come about?" He said that with the draft, the minute he graduated he was going to be in the service, and he wanted to fly and be in the Navy, so he just signed up.

With Tim being in the military during a time of war, I began feeling remorse about being so strict with him when he was growing up. While he was in officer training school in Pensacola, Florida, he called me one evening. While we were talking, I mentioned that I had been too hard on him while he was growing up. He replied, "Mom, mom, don't ever feel that way. If I hadn't come from a home with lots of discipline I couldn't make it here. They're dropping out like flies, and I have a grown man sleeping next to me crying himself to sleep every night. So don't ever feel bad."

Life as a Single Woman

I was so grateful to my friends at Stater Brothers who helped me through this lonely time. We hung out together much of the time. Most of us ate lunch at a little restaurant two blocks down the street. I became acquainted with the owners and their daughter, Judy, and the one waitress that worked for them, Leila. We became friends. Leila and I both lived alone, so one day we decided to become roommates and rented one of the duplexes beside Stater Brothers. Leila and I lived together the last year and a half that I worked for Stater Brothers.

One morning, sitting at the breakfast table looking out the picture window in the living room, which overlooked the swimming pool, there was a Japanese gardener grooming the grounds. Leila said, "Brown, do you think we'll ever meet a man that can support us in the manner to which we have become accustomed?" It was really a nice duplex—fireplace, two bedrooms, two baths. There was just one problem. I liked a bath, so I took the one with the tub, and Leila took the one with the shower. I would soak in my tub so long that I needed to add more hot water. Leila is in the shower and, when I turned on the hot water, Leila would hit the wall. It got really cold! Leila and I were friends for years; when I left she told me if I ever needed her she would know, and she'd be there.

Time to Leave Stater Brothers

Remember in my story my friends from the ranch, Pat and Orley Blackburn? After I left the ranch, Pat and I remained friends. She was living in Morro Bay, California, and I was living in southern California. We visited each other regularly and talked on the phone quite a lot. One time, I mentioned to her how hard the work was, being a checker at Stater Brothers. I told her I didn't think I could still do this at age 50. She suggested that I move up to her area, which had a small store and markets, and she assured me I could find work. I thought that sounded pretty good, so I made the move. I hated to leave Stater Brothers.

After five years I had accumulated enough household belongings to fill a house. So one day off I drove up to Morro Bay, and Pat and I shopped around for a house. I found a two-bedroom house, unfurnished of course, and I rented it. Then I went back, called the moving van and moved everything up to Grover City, close to Morro Bay. Shortly afterward, I found a job at Safeway in Pismo Beach, working as a checker. However, the job was much easier, due to the fact that there were so many senior citizens in the area that didn't buy grocery carts full of food. They came to the store every couple of days and bought just what they needed for a day or two. It was a social hour for those senior citizens! Even though I worked a 40-hour work week, it was much easier.

Kenneth Dies

Shortly after I went to work at Safeway, on one of my days off I had gone into San Luis Obispo shopping. On my way home I stopped at Safeway to do my weekly grocery shopping. The assistant manager came up to me and said that I had a telephone call, long distance. I asked how that was possible because Safeway was an unlisted number. He said he had left a note on my door at home with the message. I asked for just the area code and he didn't remember. I knew that if I had the area code, it was one of two things: either Tim's plane had crashed or Kenneth had died. When I got home and read the note, the area code was 602, Arizona. I knew Kenneth had died.

So off I go to Arizona to take care of the ranch and meet Tim there so he could take care of all the funeral arrangements. The first thing I did was meet Dr. Arnold in Kingman about my shoulder. I told him Kenneth had passed, and I needed some time off to take care of things at the ranch because Tim didn't have much time off, as he was in the service. I told Dr. Arnold I had a little bump on my shoulder and wondered if he could take it off and let me apply for workman's compensation. He said it was no problem, to go up to the hospital and get checked in for surgery. He fixed my shoulder and told me to let him know when I was ready to go back to work and he would release me. This allowed me to continue receiving paychecks and pay my bills back home while out of work and taking care of things in Arizona.

Tim took on the responsibility for the funeral arrangements and told me not to worry about anything; he would take care of it. Tim asked me if his dad had said anything about what kind of arrangements he wanted. I told him that Kenneth and I had talked it over, and Kenneth wanted a closed casket and the cheapest funeral money could buy, and he wanted to be buried in a military cemetery. He didn't want money spent on the dead, save it for the living! So when Tim went to the mortuary, the mortician tried to sell him more expensive caskets. But Tim told him, "I want the cheapest thing you have." And the mortician said "No, you have to honor your father, you should have something nicer." Tim told him he was honoring his father's wishes by choosing the least expensive option, because that's what his father wanted. Tim was only allowed five days leave; he flew back to Mississippi to continue his flight training in the Navy.

Don Dedara Calls

In 1971, when Kenneth passed, as I said before, I was at the ranch cleaning it up to sell. The phone rang, and it was Don Dedara. I was so surprised to hear from him. I said, "Don, I haven't heard from you in over six years. How are you?" He said, "I have had you and Hidden Valley on my mind for over three days. I feel that something is wrong and I had to make the call." I told him yes, Kenneth just died. He said, "I knew there was something wrong." This is one of several things that have happened in my life that I can't explain. Not only his phone call, but also the fact that I was at the ranch when the call came in.

How Kenneth Had Changed

After the funeral I had a long talk with Wayne Gallatin, Kenneth's boss. He said, "I have never seen such a change in a man as with Kenneth. Kenneth's brain was like a sponge, absorbing knowledge at incredible amounts." Wayne told me the story about the time he put some work material on the desk and told Kenneth that the company was making some changes and needed him to look this material over. Kenneth's reply was, "What do you want me to do, homework?" Wayne said he should have fired him a long time ago, but he just couldn't do it. Wayne realized the excessive drinking was causing a change in Kenneth, not only at work but also at home. But Wayne liked him and Kenneth had been with the company for ten years and did a good job. I told Wayne I should never have left Kenneth, and maybe if I had stayed things would have been different. Wayne assured me that if I had stayed, we would be having two funerals instead of one.

Cleaning Up the Ranch

So I spent 30 days cleaning and painting the ranch and preparing it for sale. I had been gone only six years, but they (Kenneth and his new wife) had destroyed the place. It was filthy. The pump on the well had gone out, and we had to carry water quite a ways to the house. We couldn't use the bathroom because of no water, so we had to use the privy. The furnace had gone out in the house, so I called for the part and, due to a nationwide trucking strike, they wouldn't guarantee a prompt delivery. It took two weeks. We had to chop wood for the fireplace to keep warm. My mom had met me at the ranch to help out, and during this time celebrated her 65th birthday. She made the comment that she "hadn't gone very far in life. I started out carrying water from the well, using the privy and chopping wood and I'm still doing it today."

I sold the ranch by the end of the 30 days and went back home to California.

As I was putting the key in the door back home at Pismo Beach, the phone rang. It was Leila and she said, "What's going on Brown?" And I said, "How did you know?" She said I told you I would know when something was wrong. I told her Kenneth had died, and I had gone back to the ranch to tie up loose ends and bury him, and that leaving the ranch the second time was almost as hard as it was the first time.

I Start Dating!

While I was working at Stater Brothers I never dated, as I was always hanging out with my friends from the job. After I moved, I got to know my next door neighbors, Ruth and Bob. They were from Texas. They had a nephew and his name was Gene Page. He was a college professor in Texas, but he was coming to our area to teach a summer course in geography at Cal Poly University. Ruth told me I had to meet her nephew. I met Gene, and since we got along real well and liked each other, we dated the entire summer of 1970. Gene had never been married, and was a confirmed bachelor and an adventurous soul. Before I met him he had built a sailboat and sailed to Hawaii. He circled the islands and sold his sailboat and then flew home. When he left at the end of our summer and went back to Texas, he had already planned a trip he wanted to take. He wanted to ride a motorcycle to the tip of South America. He really was a fun person and I thoroughly enjoyed the summer with him.

After Gene left at the end of the summer, I decided the house I was renting was too big; I thought I would like a mobile home. So I bought one. It was a single wide and I just loved it! The mobile home park was behind Safeway and so close I could go home for lunch.

After I dated Gene, I dated Bob. Bob was one of my customers and, since we weren't all that busy in the store, I had time to talk with my customers as they came through my line. He was a lieutenant at the men's colony, which was a prison located near San Luis Obispo. He asked me one day if I fished. I told him, "I love it," and he said, "Let's go one of these days." So we started dating. Bob was fresh out of a divorce and had the attitude of "poor me, she didn't understand me, she found somebody else," etc. This I did not need, so I broke it off.

Then I dated Don Young. Don was one of my customers at Safeway.

One day when we were talking, we discovered we lived in the same mobile home park. He wanted to know what space I was in, and when I told him he said, "Oh, you're the one that took the space I wanted." Don and I became real good friends. But it didn't go very far as I met Glyn Watts!

I Meet Glyn

    Bob Cates was the manager of the meat department at work. He told me one day he had the right man for me, his brother-in-law, Glyn Watts. I asked about his dating status and Bob said this man was getting a divorce. I asked how long he had been single, and Bob said two months! Since I had been there and done that with the Bob I had dated before, I was not interested. I said, "If your brother-in-law is still single in a year or two, I might date him." Bob was persistent. He said if any two people belong together, it's you and Glyn. From that day on, Bob was on my back. Bob said, "We are going bowling Saturday night, and I want you to come meet my brother-in-law." I told Bob, "I don't want to meet your brother-in-law." Bob kept it up. First it was going fishing, then to a BBQ at my brother-in-law's house. On and on, he kept it up.

    Finally, he told me his wife was cooking dinner on Sunday night, and when his wife cooks dinner and invites people over, they accept and come and eat! He was inviting his brother-in-law as well, and if I didn't come, he would come over to my house and carry me to his house, so my hair better be combed!! And he would have done it too! Knowing Bob, he would have given me a hell of a bad time if I didn't show! A couple of nights before the date, I was talking on the phone with my friend, Laura. I told her I have a blind date on Sunday night and you may know the guy, he owns the Foster's Freeze in San Luis Obispo. Laura asked, "Glyn Watts?" And I said, "Yes, that's his name." She said, "Nancy you go on that date. Bob and I just love Glyn; he is a wonderful person." So I felt better about going on the date.

First Date and Marrying Glyn

So Sunday night rolled around and I showed up in my little red sports car, a Triumph TR-4, and Glyn showed up in a baby blue Corvette. Glyn and I hit it off right away. There was definite chemistry and it was love at first sight! He was 45 and I was 43. We laughed a lot and started dating immediately, and quickly fell in love. We were crazy about each other and spent all of our time together. I don't know how we did it, but we waited nine days before we had sex. And boy, it was worth the wait!!

Glyn had also joined the Navy at age 17. He went aboard the aircraft carrier USS Intrepid and went through many battles during WWII.

Glyn had a bad marriage of 24 years and he never talked about his marriage. I had had a very good marriage that had turned bad. We met on February 28, 1971 and his divorce wasn't final until August 17th, 1971. We were married on that same day, August 17, 1971. I used to tell friends that when I married Glyn, I had died and gone to heaven.

Glyn had bought a home just before we met. We remodeled that home and lived there for our first five years of marriage. At the end of the five years we had started to do some traveling. So we sold the house and bought a triple-wide mobile home, because it needed no upkeep like the house.

Tim Meets Betz

In the Navy, Tim's job was flying F-4 jets. He loved it and was on cloud nine; he knew this is where he wanted to be. But the Navy decided they had too many jet pilots, so they called a meeting and said, "Look at the man on your left and the man on your right. When this meeting is over, only one of the three of you will still be in the Navy." They passed out the envelopes and the man on Tim's left was out. The man on Tim's right was out also. So Tim thought he had a pretty good chance. He opened his envelope and he was still in the Navy, BUT he was no longer flying. They put him on a desk job in Okinawa, Japan.

One night he was at the Officers Club with one of his buddies when these two girls walked in. Tim told his buddy, "I'll take the blonde." But before he could make a move an Air Force man stepped in, and made a move. The woman turned out to be Betty Winter. He told his buddy, "I don't think that blonde is having too good a time over there. I think I'll go over and ask her to dance." Then he said to his buddy, "Give me 6 o'clock," (which in Navy terms means cover my back). From that night on, Tim and Betty were dating. Betty put in for a teaching job overseas and had been chosen; that's how she got to Okinawa. She had military rights, same as Tim, so they hitchhiked on military planes to Shanghai, Singapore, and pretty much all over the Far East. When it was time for Tim to come home, and Betty as well, they decided to get married after their time in Okinawa was over.

Tim Returns to the States with Betz

They came home from Okinawa in March of 1972. Tim came home a couple of days ahead of Betty, and Glyn and I drove up to Fairfield Airport to pick Tim up. He stayed a couple of nights with us and it was so wonderful to have Tim back in my life!! Then he drove back to the airport to pick up Betty. Since they were so close to Oregon, they drove up to Bend to visit his dad's family. They came back to San Luis Obispo, and we loaded up the RV and boat and took off for a fishing trip to Arizona. We camped for five days and then took Betty to Las Vegas for her to catch a plane to Minnesota to plan the wedding. Glyn took the boat and RV back to San Luis Obispo, and Tim and I drove across country to Minnesota.

They were married on March 11, 1972. It was very special to us, since we had just been married seven months before, in August 1971. After the wedding, they put me on a plane back to California, and then drove across country to El Paso, Texas, to visit Tim's dad's grave.

Becoming Friends with Betz

I hit it off with Betty from the beginning. She became my best friend. I have always been thankful Tim chose her for his wife. Since Glyn's first wife's name was Betty, and he was very bitter about the marriage, it didn't take long for Glyn to hang a new nickname on Betty; thus she became known as "Betz," even to Tim. The four of us became very close. Almost every weekend we did stuff together—fishing, camping, playing tennis, watching hot air balloons. To my surprise, Glyn's three kids developed some jealousy, and we were told not to talk about Tim and Betz. Glyn and I were very happy, so we decided to ignore their demands.

Starting Work at the Foster's Freeze

After Glyn and I were married, I did the wifely thing and stayed home until the first of November. I had been used to working, so I asked Glyn if I could work with him at the Foster's Freeze. He was so happy for us to work together. On November 1, 1971 I went to work at the Foster's Freeze with Glyn; from that day on we were together 24/7. The only time we were apart was when he went to get a haircut or I went to the beauty shop or for doctor appointments. When he came home from the doctor's office, he could never remember what the doctor told him. It would take him up to three days and he would always say, "Oh yea, the doctor also said blah blah blah." After that, I started going to the doctor with him so I could get the information firsthand.

We were married 42 years, and not once did we ever raise our voices at each other. We never had an argument. I said to Tim one day, "Glyn and I had an argument, and I want you to settle it." Tim said, "Mom, you and Glyn may have had a discussion, but you didn't have an argument."

A Lot in Common

We both loved to hunt, fish and camp, and to shop. When I got ready to go shopping he would always say,

"Wait 'til I get my hat." Glyn always wore a hat, ranging from straw hats and safari hats to cowboy hats and baseball caps. We loved to take trips, we liked the same movies and TV shows, we liked the same people, and we were both staunch Republicans. Our sexual desire for each other was equally matched, and that lasted through the entire 42 years of marriage! As Bob said, if two people ever deserved to be together, it was me and Glyn.

Glyn's Family – Good Friends

Glyn was an only child. His mother had such a hard time delivering that his dad said he would never put his wife through that again. Glyn's dad had eight sisters and brothers. They all had come from Texas, and caravanned together from Texas to California during the Depression. Since I had spent most of my childhood in Arkansas, I fit right in and was good friends with all of them.

Glyn had three grown children. Pam, the oldest, was married and had a baby boy named Jimmy. Jane was 11 months younger than Pam and never married or had children. Mitch was the youngest and was three years younger than Jane, had married four times and had two boys by his first wife. Shortly after Glyn and I got married, Pam divorced her husband, and Mitch had moved out on his own away from home. I have told you about the way I have raised Tim, how he had turned out to be very independent, but these three kids had no desire for higher education, though their grandmother would have paid for it willingly

Leaving on our honeymoon

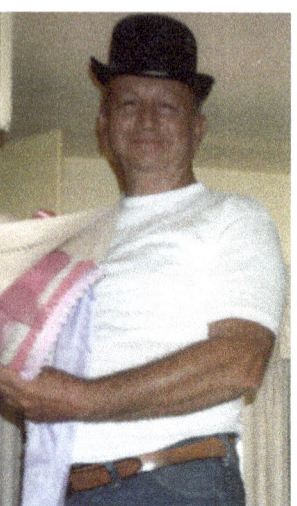
Glyn, the life of the party

I was a bag of popcorn at Stater Brothers Halloween.

Glyn always had fun.

Glyn making us laugh

Never apart

Christmas with the kids

Glyn

Glyn's Mother Rowena

so she could have bragged to her friends and family of her grandchildren's accomplishments. They had been handed everything from grandma and grandpa. For example, when Jane was in her 50's, she would call grandma when her car license came due and ask her grandma for money for the payment.

Pam's Sense of Entitlement

Glyn's mom, Rowena, called up one day and told Glyn that since Pam is living on her own and her former husband, John, is not paying any more child support, Pam had called grandma and said she didn't have enough money to buy milk for the baby. So grandma said, "I'm going to send money from my social security check." Pam's mother is giving her money, so grandma asked Glyn if he could give Pam $200 to $300 dollars every month to help her out. Glyn, of course, agreed. Pam came down to the store one morning to visit her dad and when she started to leave, she cleaned the garbage out of her car and threw it in the garbage can in the kitchen. Later I was putting something in the garbage can and I saw Pam's garbage. There were three copies of *Playgirl* @ $2.75/copy. I said, "She doesn't have money to buy milk for the baby, but she has money for this smut!!" I called Glyn over to come to the kitchen and showed him the magazines. He could not believe Pam had done such a thing, and he said, "I don't think I should give her money." He wanted to take her down to Safeway anytime she needed groceries and fill the basket. He said he would make arrangements with Stan and Dale, who owned the service station across the street from Foster's Freeze, to get gas and repairs for her car. He called Pam and asked her to come down to the store for a moment. Glyn and I were standing in the kitchen talking when she walked in. He told her what he had told me of the arrangements he had made. If looks could kill, I would have died on the spot. Pam knew exactly where this had come from.

Getting Along with Glyn's Family

Glyn's wife was as bad as the kids. She would say to Glyn's folks, "I wish we had a better car; everyone in the neighborhood has a nicer car than we have." She was driving a little Ford Tempest. So Glyn's folks went down and made a down payment on a Pontiac Chieftain. Now Glyn had a car payment, higher insurance and paying more for gas. The same thing happened when the kids decided they wanted a swimming pool. Grandma and grandpa put in a swimming pool, which added to Glyn's monthly utility payments. Again, the kids wanted horses, so grandma and grandpa bought three horses; now Glyn was paying vet bills and buying hay. They were killing him with kindness. The sad part of the story was that all of the Watts family had been told of all the great things they had done for Glyn. I had become a very independent person in my lifetime. Having been on my own a couple of times, I made up my mind there would be no more stories like this about Glyn and me.

Needless to say, there was a lot of trouble between Glyn's mother and me. I refused to accept any financial help from them. Through the years, the only thing I ever accepted from her was Christmas presents. I told her Glyn was my husband and Glyn will support me and take care of me. We don't need your money. After that we didn't speak for eight years. It all worked out and we became very close before she passed away.

It was sad what happened between her and Glyn's children. She turned all of her finances over to Glyn's cousin, Wanda, for her to handle. From that point forward, all requests for money went through Wanda. Wanda closed the purse strings.

One day Mitch called Rowena and asked for $30,000. She told him that Wanda was now in charge of the finances and to talk to Wanda. So he called Wanda and asked for the money. Wanda asked for collateral because she saw it as a loan. Mitch said he didn't need collateral because this was his grandmother's money and it should be given to him free and clear, not in the form of a loan.

At this time, Glyn and I had been married 19 years. In those 19 years, Glyn's kids had visited us one time. Glyn got a call from Mitch saying he's coming for a visit. Glyn asked, "Please just let him come to see me and not put the bite on me." Mitch came with his two sons, David and Kevin. They stayed for three days. On the third day, Mitch said, "Come on dad, let's go to the store and buy some stuff for the kids to eat on the way home." When they came out of the store, in the parking lot, he put the bite on Glyn for $30,000. Glyn told him he didn't have that kind of money and, besides, it was invested for retirement. Mitch then asked if I could loan him the money, since my mom left me money when she died, and Glyn told him absolutely no way would he ask for money from me to give to Mitch. I don't know if Mitch ever found anyone to lend him the $30,000, but his search certainly ended with us.

When Glyn eventually died, he was very sad, frustrated and bitter about the way his kids had turned out and how they treated us. Glyn was not a man to ever cuss, but he told me to "never give those kids a goddamn dime." And I never did.

CHAPTER SIX

The Foster's Freeze Years

The Purchase Of Foster's Freeze

Back in 1946, one of Glyn's cousins asked Glyn's dad, Mac, to loan him the money to start a new business, a Foster's Freeze. He gave him the money, and the cousin paid it back in 14 months. Glyn's dad thought this must be a pretty good business, so he decided to buy a lot, build the building in the town of Porterville, California, and buy the franchise. Up to this time Glyn had been working as a painter for his dad, but his dad decided to put him in the Foster's Freeze to run it.

The Foster's Freeze turned out to be a real money maker. So Glyn's dad decided to build another Foster's Freeze on some land he had leased In San Luis Obispo. Mac put his own brother in the Foster's Freeze in San Luis Obispo. The Foster's Freeze in San Luis Obispo turned out not to be the money maker that the others were. Mac realized his brother didn't have the personality to meet the public. Mac told Glyn, "If you'll move to San Luis Obispo and manage the Foster's Freeze, I will give you half interest." So in 1952

Glyn moved his family to San Luis Obispo and ran the Foster's Freeze for 30 years, retiring in 1982.

Updating the Foster's Freeze

The Foster's Freeze was built in 1948, and nothing had been done to the building since that date. Mac never believed in putting any money in the Foster's Freeze; he was very tight with his money. It drove me crazy, it needed updating so bad. Glyn and I talked it over, and he said he had wanted to update it for years. But his dad wouldn't let go of the money to make the necessary remodeling changes.

About that time new management took over the headquarters of Foster's Freeze, and they were all for remodeling all the old stores. They came up with the idea of putting mansards on the roof. We went over to see Mac and Glyn told him about the mansards and said he wanted to put one on the Foster's Freeze. Mac didn't think it was necessary because only so many cars will go past that store, and only so many will stop, and even if you put a gold dome on top it wouldn't increase your business one bit! So on the way home Glyn said, "I don't care what dad said, I'm putting the mansards on."

Buying Glyn's Dad Out of the Foster's Freeze

This was the first time Glyn had defied his father; he had always done everything his dad told him to do. Glyn and I decided we were going to put a lot of money into the Foster's Freeze to bring it up to date, and with that in mind, we wanted his name off the title. We wanted to own it outright. Glyn called his dad and told him that we are going to be putting a lot of money into the Foster's Freeze and we want to buy your half interest. That went over like a fart in church. His dad came up with the figure of $50,000. I said to Glyn to go over and talk to Jimmy, the manager of the bank, and we'll sell the house and we'll pay the $50,000. Mac told us we could pay the $50,000 when we retire and sell the Foster's Freeze. We refused this offer because it wouldn't work for our retirement plans. We never went to the bank. Mac came back with another plan: $200 per month until he and Rowena both died. So in 1973 we decided to buy the Foster's Freeze from his dad. Mac died in 1981 and she didn't die until 2000, so the total ended up being $64,800! We never missed a payment.

The Big Remodel Begins

Now that we had clear title to the Foster's Freeze, we began one of the biggest remodeling projects of all time. First, we had to install public restrooms, since there had never been restrooms for the public before. We needed another ice machine, another ice cream machine, and another French fryer. When we added the new fryer, the exhaust fan wasn't big enough to handle the extra heat, so we had to install a new one. We tore out the old refrigerator and got rid of the old chest freezers and installed a walk-in refrigerator and deep freeze. We had an open air dining room with redwood tables and benches. We enclosed the dining area and added new tables and booths. There was just one problem. With all the new machinery we had added, right in the middle of the lunch rush, the old 1948 wiring couldn't handle the load and we blew the fuses. So we had to rewire the whole building and, in addition, put heat and air conditioning in the new dining area.

Buying the Land Under the Foster's Freeze

Two years later, the lease on the land was about to expire. Glyn received a phone call from the owner of the land asking if Glyn would come to his office to talk. Glyn went over and the owner of the land asked Glyn if he was interested in buying the land under the Foster's Freeze. The price was $40,000. Glyn said yes, but let me talk to my wife and I'll get back to you. I said, "If we have to live on dry bread and branch water we're going to buy that land." So we took our savings, a mortgage and a second mortgage and bought the land. Now we owned the Foster's Freeze, land, building, franchise and all!

Looking for a Place to Retire

After the remodeling settled down, life became very routine. Like everyone else, we went to work, came home, and ate out a lot. This was our life until 1979. One of the employees, Jeanine, had worked for Glyn about 11 years and we promoted her to manager. This allowed us some well-deserved time off. We began looking for a place to retire.

A Life Well Lived

We knew we wanted out of California, so we started traveling the Northwest in our motorhome and spent about a month in each state—eastern Washington, Idaho, Montana, northern Nevada. The last state we traveled was Utah. We had quite an experience in Utah.

We were there for the hunting season in the fall and in an unfamiliar area. Glyn stopped and asked the service station attendant if there were any lakes nearby, and the guy said there was Panguitch Lake up the mountain. It was raining but we thought nothing of it. But the further up the mountain we went, it turned to snow! It was snowing so hard that it was hard to tell exactly where the road was. We traveled quite a ways and came to a point in the road where there was a car stopped due to poor visibility. Glyn went up and talked to the guy in the car and it was a couple, Hazel and Matt Housman, on their way to Cedar City for supplies for their restaurant. Hazel came back to our motorhome and said that, when a storm comes in, they close the gate at the bottom of the mountain to prevent people from getting stuck in the snow, so now no one knows we're up here. Glyn had insisted we have a CB Radio (Citizens Band) in our motorhome, and I didn't like it. It was just a bunch of truckers taking back and forth. Anyway, I told Hazel we have a CB radio, and she said, "Get on it, and call for help!" So I called "Breaker 1-9, breaker 1-9," but no response. So I told Hazel I'm going on mayday alert, but again no response. We sat there a while and, again, I tried calling for help, and suddenly there was a response. I told him there were five cars stuck in the snow on Panguitch Mountain. I turned to Hazel and said, "Where are we?" She said, "We're one mile from where they tore down the old lodge."

Next thing you know, here comes a big snow cat and he called for help. Help arrived in the form of a road grader, which did nothing, so then they sent up a bulldozer. Meanwhile, I had 12 people in my motorhome. There was a man who had been stationed in England; he was on his way to Nellis Air Force Base in Las Vegas. He and his wife had two kids with them. With another couple, the man was a pit boss in Vegas. He and his wife had been there since 9:00 a.m. and all he had to remove the snow from the tailpipe was a Styrofoam ice chest top. His wife was so upset she was vomiting. She thought they were going to die because they couldn't run the car with the heater because he couldn't get the snow away from the tailpipe.

So by 4:00 p.m., they had the road cleared and a ranger came by and warned us to get off the mountain. They were expecting 100 mile per hour winds that night. The pit boss was wearing jeans and a plaid shirt and looked like a regular guy. He told us that if anybody makes it to Vegas tonight, steak and lobster was on him! Glyn and I made it as far as St. George, Utah. The next day we made it to Vegas and stopped to say hello to the pit boss. When we walked in and saw him, he looked just like the mafia—in a black suit! He yelled out in the casino, "These are the people that saved my life!" He took us over to the restaurant, and there was a very long line. So he walked up to the head of the line, dropped the rope, and told the waitress to seat Mr. and Mrs. Watts, which she did. He joined us for breakfast, and we had a great time.

We Move to Utah

In our search for a retirement place, we drove through many beautiful valleys in Montana and Idaho. I told Glyn we couldn't live there, there's nobody there but Mormons, and hell, I wouldn't last five minutes with the Mormons. I smoke, I drink, and I cuss. So where did we settle??? Utah—ground zero for Mormons!

We headed back to California and worked the Foster's Freeze through the winter months. When the weather warmed up we loaded up the motorhome, hooked up the Bronco, put a small boat on top of the Bronco, and headed for Utah. We planned to spend some time at Panquitch Lake before touring Utah. We were at the lake for several days and I got sick. We went down to the town of Panquitch to the doctor, and he said he thought I had altitude sickness, because it's 8,500 feet high at the lake. Glyn went back to the lake, hooked up everything and came back down to Panquitch.

We Discover Beaver, Utah

We were in a campground, so we got out the map and started to find the next stop. We saw that there was a lake called Minersville close to the town of Beaver, which has

Glyn and I always worked together.

Our Foster's Freeze

Working in the Foster's Freeze kitchen

IN CALIFORNIA AFTER HONEYMOON— Mr. and Mrs. Tim Brown (Betty Winter) are now in LeMoore, California following their wedding March 11th at Our Savior's Lutheran Church in Dovray.

The announcement of Tim and Betz's marriage

Tim and Betz

an elevation of 6,500 feet. When we came into Beaver, Glyn said, "I'm going to cut the Bronco loose, and you go do the grocery shopping." He would go out and set up camp at the lake. I went to the store, and right away I knew we had found the right place to live. It was like stepping back in time 30 or 40 years, like it had been in Oatman. The store sold guns, ammo, saddles, and horse shoes. The grocery section had a meat counter and a very small produce section. There were wood floors and a tin ceiling. I got my groceries and drove out to the lake. I told Glyn, "Eureka, I have found it!"

The next day we drove into town and he said, "You're right babe, this is it." We found a real estate agent, and the first place he took us was love at first sight. It was a big grove of cottonwood trees with a river nearby. We bought an acre and a half, and sealed the deal over the hood of a pickup truck with a handshake. We had water and electric brought to the property and moved the RV there. Since Beaver was 6,500 feet, it was snow country. So time to build was short. We bought the property on June 1st, and by July we were building. We contacted a contractor who was recommended by a man from the lumber company. We told him we wanted a log cabin. He told us he could build a cabin in 65 days, but would rather say 90 days. In this small town, it took only a short time to have plans drawn up. I don't remember even having to have a building permit. We started the foundation by the middle of July, and the contractor turned out to be the contractor from hell! Five and a half months later, at the end of December, the cabin was finished. Glyn and I, along with the contractor, sat at the kitchen table for three days, arguing about the final payment. We refused to make the payment until he signed a paper stating that all the outstanding bills against the cabin had been paid, and he would be responsible for any incoming bills from that point on. He finally signed.

Introduction to Black Meadow

We left the cabin January 2, 1980 and went back, intending to work at the Foster's Freeze for the winter. Around the first of February, we were getting antsy to go someplace. My mom and Slim, my stepdad who I loved dearly, had been by for a visit. He was talking about a place where his brother was living that was called Black Meadow. It was an old fishing camp on Lake Havasu. After they went home, Glyn and I decided to take a trip down to this lake. Slim was right; it was a very old camp but the fishing was very good. We stayed until the middle of April and then took off for the cabin in Utah.

Our First Summer in our Beaver, Utah Cabin

It was so good to be back at the cabin. We had made a lot of friends in the grove the summer before. We planted a big garden with a very high fence to keep the deer out. Glyn had never gardened before. His Aunt Mattie always said that Glyn was really an old country boy at heart. I never knew how true that was until we planted the garden.

The garden grew so much we had to can a lot. We had no place to put all that we had canned, so we dug a cellar under the house. It was so much fun to go down in the cellar and see all that we had canned. We caught, canned and smoked fish. The summer went by so fast. All of our neighbors were summer homes. We had a big farewell party and everyone was so sad to leave.

We lived in that log cabin for eleven summers until 1990. We met our best friends who lived next door to the cabin, Chuck and Ellie Freislinger, in 1979 when we were camped at Minersville Lake. They had said to each other that they knew me from somewhere but couldn't place me. One evening Ellie walked over to our camp and asked if we would like to join their campfire. Come to find out they remembered me from Stater Brothers. They most often went in Betty Walker's line, as they were her next door neighbors. The next summer they came to the cabin for a two week vacation. They ended up buying the lot next door to our cabin, where they built a log cabin. Chuck eventually died in 2006 from brain cancer. Ellie put the cabin up for sale in 2011 and it finally sold in 2016.

Going Back to Black Meadow

At the end of summer, we left the cabin and headed for Black Meadow. By the end of the winter we had bought a 40 foot travel trailer with an Arizona room. Now we were set. Summers in the cabin were 80-85 degrees, and winters in Black Meadow were 50-80 degrees.

We had owned boats, but now we bought our first pontoon. On nice winter days we would go out on the lake and live on the pontoon for three to four days. There were campsites all up and down the lake and they had porta-potties, fire pits, and tables. It was the middle of winter and we had the whole lake to ourselves.

Selling Foster's Freeze

In 1982, we decided to sell the Foster's Freeze. Glyn had worked and managed the Foster's Freeze, except for a short time, since 1952. Thirty years. He called the owner of the Foster's Freeze in Morro Bay, California, Dale, and asked him if he would like to buy the San Luis Obispo store. Dale had always wanted to buy our location, so he said yes. We made the deal to sell the building and franchise, but we kept the land.

When I went to work at the Foster's Freeze in 1971, the gross take was between $60 and $70 thousand a year. After the remodel and when we sold, the gross take was almost $450,000 per year.

The next years were pretty uneventful. Cabin in the summer, lake in the winter. Life was good. Glyn was a joy to live with; he always made me laugh. If I had one word to describe him, it would be "mischievous." My memory escapes me right now, and I can't think of any examples, but there were many. It was just his way. He would get a twinkle in his eye and I just knew that something was going to happen. He was so much fun!

CHAPTER SEVEN

Moving Around in the Retirement Years

Tim and Betz Give Us Grandchildren!!

After Tim and Betz were married in 1972, Tim stayed in the Navy and they were assigned to Lemoore Naval Air Base. When he left the Navy they settled in the little town of Lemoore, California. Betz went back to teaching school at the Air Base. She taught for 34 years and then retired. We became a close, loving family.

After Tim and Betz had been married for five years, they blessed us with our first grandchild, Dana Rhea Brown, in 1977. Glyn and I went over and stayed for two weeks to help with the housework and baby Dana. Three years later, we were blessed again with our second granddaughter, Anne Jenee Brown. And finally, three years later, we were blessed once more with our third granddaughter, Lynn DeAnne Brown.

At the time of this writing, summer 2017, the granddaughters are all grown up. Tim and Betz did a wonderful job raising those girls. Tim paid to put all three girls through college and the girls worked to pay their living expenses.

Glyn and I really enjoyed the years together, watching these girls grow up and sharing in all the fun times—camping, fishing, trips, hiding Easter eggs and all those wonderful Christmases. They grew into beautiful young women that we are very proud of, and I treasure all those times spent with them!

Granddaughters – Where Are They Now?
Dana

Dana is a paralegal, Anne is a part-time Algebra teacher and part-time in Administration. Lynn is also working in the same law office as Dana. Dana married her husband, Pete Mullin, in 2004. Pete works in a courtroom as a bailiff for the sheriff's department. They have two beautiful children, Matthew Nicholas Mullin, born May 2006, and Kara Ann Mullin, born February 2010.

Anne

While in college, Anne got pregnant and kept the baby. The baby, Kadin Lee Brown, was born April 2004. Anne gave him the surname of Brown because she was single, and her father always wanted a boy to carry on the Brown name. She eventually met and married her husband, Jerod Strong, and they had a child together, Skylar Ann Strong, born April 2008. Jerod is an eighth grade math teacher.

Lynn

Lynn is having a hard time finding her niche in life. I

have faith she will find it and, when she does, she will say it was worth the wait. She is back in college working on her Master's Degree.

The Passing of our Fathers

In 1980, my stepdad, Slim, passed away at age 83. His going was peaceful. My mother became a widow and accepted her new life. She had lots of friends, was 73 years old and very active. In 1981, Glyn's dad, Mac, passed away, leaving Glyn's mother, Rowena, a very wealthy woman. She was 71.

Black Meadow to Topock

We loved being at the lake. We had so many friends and had such good times. In early 1984, the management of the camp changed. The new manager was the manager from hell! We knew we needed to move. We bought a lot in Topock, Arizona, overlooking the marsh.

This spot was very dear to me. It was only about 25 to 30 miles from the old ranch where Tim, Kenneth and I had lived. We had a camper that we took off the truck and put in a camping spot. We spent many days and nights camping and fishing the marsh. I never mentioned all of this to Glyn, because he was extremely jealous of Kenneth, even though I had told him over and over that he had no reason to be jealous. Maybe you noticed that when Glyn and I were looking for a place to retire, we never even considered Oregon, because Kenneth and I lived in Oregon in the

1940's. Yet Glyn was alright with living in Arizona. It wasn't rational, but it was just the way he was.

Glyn and I bought a single wide mobile home and put it on the lot. This was our winter home while spending summers in Beaver at the cabin. When we lived on the marsh, we were close to Bullhead City, Arizona and Laughlin, Nevada. We started going to the casinos in Laughlin, because we both loved gambling and the food. It was in 1984, and we continued gambling the rest of our married lives. We would lose a little and win a little, and had hours of fun alone and with friends.

What can I say about our lives at this time? We remodeled or built every home we had owned, even the travel trailer and the mobile home. We took trips, spent time with our family and went fishing.

Glyn's Heart Attack

In March of 1990 we were living our carefree life. Then, Glyn woke me up one morning at 3:00 a.m. He was having chest pains, so I drove him to the emergency room in Needles, California. They got him stabilized and flew him to Phoenix. I went home and called Tim. In the six years I was single, Tim had become my strength. I told him about Glyn and that he was in Phoenix. I said I hadn't driven much in the 19 years we had been married because Glyn did all the driving. Driving in Phoenix would be like driving in Los Angeles. Tim said, "Get in the goddamn car and drive." I said, "Okay, I will."

I made the trip to Phoenix just fine and drove Glyn home from the hospital. He was in ICU for three days and the hospital for four more days. He was put on a diet and told to lose weight and exercise. Glyn's weight went down from 238 to 212. He never weighed more than 212 for the rest of his life. We did this for two years, and then gradually slipped back into our old ways.

Selling Topock and Beaver and Buying the House at Lake Havasu

We talked things over and knew there had to be a lot of changes. We realized we could no longer have both homes. Glyn said if anything happened to him I couldn't live in Beaver alone, continue the maintenance and travel between two homes. And the mobile home in Topock would be way too hot to stay in during the summers. You can't live in one in temperatures of 120 degrees. He wanted to put me in a home where I could live year 'round and in a town. We had always lived in the woods or desert, so this would be quite an adjustment.

We decided to sell the cabin in Beaver and the mobile home in Topock and buy a house in Lake Havasu. We contacted a contractor and told him that we wanted a house with good thick insulation, a home with R-40 in the ceilings and R-30 in the walls. He said they were already building homes like that in Lake Havasu. It was really a sad time and a hard thing to do. We bought a lot in Havasu and drew up the plans. A three bedroom, two bath Spanish style, with a tile roof, tile floors in the dining room, kitchen and baths. The contractor gave us our own girl to work with and take care of everything. Her name was Sheri and we became very close to her. We picked the floor plan, all the colors for tile, walls and carpet, and left to spend the summer in the cabin. We only visited the building site once. We came down to Havasu when they were putting in the insulation because we wanted to be sure we had the R-40 and R-30. Other than that, we didn't see the house until fall. When we walked in the door, the home was exactly the way it was supposed to be. It was beautiful.

The Beaver cabin had sold and it was so sad to see it go. The mobile hadn't sold yet, but it only took a few months to sell. It was paid for, so we didn't have two mortgages. The house in Havasu was a house to die for. We built a kiva fireplace, put in a swimming pool and Jacuzzi. We built stucco walls around the lot. When summer came, it was to be our first summer in Havasu. With a three ton air conditioner and a pool, it wasn't too bad.

Pat and Don and Building the Cabin Near Flagstaff

As I mentioned before, Chuck and Ellie were originally from Chicago. They had a couple they had grown up with in Chicago, Pat and Don, who moved to California the same time Chuck and Ellie did. We met Pat and Don, who had moved to Havasu about the same time Glyn and I did, and became very close friends. There wasn't a day that would go by when I didn't call Pat or she called me. We had dinner at each other's homes, went to lunch, and to the casinos. As the second summer rolled around, we weren't happy—thinking about how hot the car was, the fact that you didn't go shopping until 9:00 or 10:00 p.m. because of the heat. No outside activities except swimming. The way of life was much like living in cold country, no activities outside. (That was then; now people ski and enjoy cold weather outdoor activities.)

One day I called Pat and said, "Let's go up to Flagstaff and rent a condo for the summer." She said, "Count me in." There was just one problem. All the people from Phoenix had already gone there for summer; there was not a condo to be found. Every real estate office we visited said the same thing, no condos, but we have lots of land. When we got home from Flagstaff, I asked Glyn about buying some land and building another log cabin. He said, "Yeah, these summers are awfully hot." I picked up the phone and called Tim and asked him about going in half on a log cabin in Flagstaff. He said, "When do we start building?" I asked Tim to go in half because things were so expensive, not like it was in the 1970's and 1980's. Glyn and I went back to Flagstaff in the RV to buy land. We had a large selection of land to choose from, so I told Tim to fly up. He turned down all the selections after seeing them. We kept looking and found 13 acres covered in pinyon pine and told Tim to fly up again to see it. He said this better be good this time. The land was 10 miles out of Williams, Arizona. When he saw the 13 acres, it was love at first sight. It was what we were looking for.

Building Our New Cabin

After what we had gone through with the contractor from hell in Beaver, I was sure I wouldn't let that happen again. So I started my search. I would be in the beauty shop with my head in the shampoo bowl and ask the lady, "If you're going to build a house, who would you get?" "Mike Bavier," she said. I asked the same question all over town and got the same answer, Mike Bavier. We contacted him and he built our cabin. It went so smooth, and the cabin turned out beautiful. It was much larger than the first cabin in Beaver.

Tim said he wanted to build all the cabinet doors in the kitchen and baths himself. It was okay with Mike. But the guy, Bob, who worked with Mike, was really upset about it. He told Mike that after all the work they had done in the cabin, letting some guy you don't even know do the doors was crazy. Mike told him Nancy said it was alright.

Mike gave us the measurements; we took them to California and handed them to Tim, who built the doors. We took the doors to Arizona and they fit perfectly and were beautiful. Bob was really impressed. Tim also built a beautiful island for the kitchen. Now we were back to two places again. This time it was a lot closer, three hours door to door.

Our "RV" Boat on Lake Powell

One day we decided to go over to Lake Powell to go fishing. While there we took a walk around the marina. The boats were all so big and beautiful. Lake Powell is a very big lake and separates Utah and Arizona. We spotted this boat with a For Sale sign, and it was a 30 foot Sea-Ray. It was like an RV, only on the water! It had the works—a bathroom, shower, air conditioning and heat, stove and fridge. We always owned an RV and a boat. I am ashamed to say how many RVs and how many boats. We upgraded continually. This was our last upgrade. The name of the boat was "Out of Control" and we were definitely out of control when we bought it. It was hell on wheels, or in this case, hell on water! We had a blast on it. Many, many hours of fun were spent on Lake Powell.

Glyn's Second Heart Attack

Around August, after we had bought the land, we contacted Mike and were waiting on him to finish a job before he could start on ours. Pat and Don and Glyn and I decided to go to Utah to visit our friends Chuck and Ellie and take a tour of Utah. We loaded up the RV and Pat and Don drove their car so we had a car to drive when we settled in to visit the sights. The first day we got as far as Winslow, Arizona. Early the next morning Glyn complained of chest pains. We took him to the ER and, sure enough, he was having a heart attack. Of all the times for one of those desert rainstorms where you get 50 percent of your annual rainfall at one time, it came up. It was 70 miles to the nearest hospital back to Flagstaff. Don drove the RV, Pat drove their car and I went in the ambulance with Glyn.

When we had Glyn in ICU being cared for, I told Pat and Don to take the RV and go ahead on vacation. I would drive their car back to Havasu. It was nice that our cars were identical. I forgot to mention that we had our cat, Heidi, with us. I went to check on her in the car and I laid my purse on the back seat and it had the code and keys to the car. When I closed the door, the car was locked! I said, "What else can go wrong?" Then the little light bulb in my head went on. When we first bought our car I took it to Pat. I told her to take off the child locks and to put a code in my car to unlock it. And she said, "If you ever forget your code, I will put your phone number in." If Pat did that to my car, I was sure she had done it to hers. I put her phone number in and click, it opened!

Glyn Has Bypass Surgery

Glynn was in ICU and hospital for four days and was told when he got home to go see his cardiologist. They put Glyn through all the tests and there was a lot of blockage in the arteries. He was to have a five-way bypass. We had to go to Las Vegas, 120 miles away, for the surgery. So that meant I was driving again. You do what you have to do. The hospitals in Vegas and Phoenix both have a service that takes care of family members. They set me up with a motel close to the hospital; the next day was the surgery.

All went well. I spent the whole day in the waiting room. When the doctor came out of surgery, he came to the waiting room and said everything was fine. When Glyn came out of surgery he went into ICU. He was still unconscious when I went in, and I had never seen so many tubes and needles. The nurse came in and said, "You have to leave. No one is allowed in here but me, the doctor, and God." The next day when I arrived at the hospital, the nurse handed me a little plastic apparatus with a ball in it. She said he is to blow the ball to the top every hour. She left the room and I never saw her again that day. At noon someone came in and brought him in some lunch. I had to leave at 4:00 p.m. so I could beat the 5:00 p.m. traffic. I stopped at the nurses' station and told them I was leaving. Tim had driven to Vegas to be with me on the second day. Glyn told Tim to take me some place to get me away from there. Tim and I went to a casino and saw the white tigers and the dolphins and had dinner. Glyn was in the hospital for a week and I took him home for his recovery.

Selling the Havasu House

We had created a big problem. The house in Havasu turned out to be a big concern because, when we were in Williams, we worried about the house and the high temperatures. We had to have a pool man, a gardener for the landscaping and someone to check on the house frequently for the air conditioning. There also were problems with the drip system. The time clock had stuck and it flooded the vacant lot next door. Luckily, our friend Don fixed it, but there was always worry about the overall maintenance of the house and grounds.

With all of this concern, it was sad, but we decided we needed to sell the house in Havasu and go condo. The condo had a pool and lots of landscaping, but they had people to take of these things, so we needn't worry. We were back to cool summers in Williams and mild winters in Havasu.

Pat Dies

At the end of the second summer, we went back to Havasu. Pat wasn't feeling good at all. It was her gall bladder. She went into surgery and they found cancer. They gave her three months to live. One day when I went to the hospital to visit her, I laid my head on the bed and cried. She said, "What are you crying about? I'm the one dying!" Three months later she was dead. It was a sad time when I lost Pat. I was thankful for all the wonderful fun times we had together. Just having her for a friend was a happy time in my life.

Beady, the Golden Years

After Pat passed, we took a trip to South Dakota to see the monuments, and took three trips to Mexico. We took one entire summer to tour Alaska in our RV. This was a trip we both wanted to take for a long time. There is a joke going around that the mosquito should be the state bird of Alaska. After spending the summer in Alaska, I can tell you it's not a joke.

One time we were in a gas station when the man on the other side of our pump said, "I wish I had your bill." He was driving a Class A motorcoach, the ones built like a Greyhound bus and getting five to six miles per gallon! We were driving our 19 foot van conversion and getting 13 to 14 miles per gallon. His wife walked by and said, "They don't have anything," and I said, "We have a complete kitchen, toilet, shower, bed and TV." She said, "Well, he can't chase you around the house." To that I said, "He doesn't have to chase me…I'm easy!!" As she walked away she didn't see the little smile on her husband's face. The following summer we took a cruise in the inland passage of Alaska to see the parts that we had missed by land.

I never found a friend to replace Pat, but I could not believe that Beady, my best friend since third grade, moved to Havasu. Beady and I had kept in touch all these years. She had spent a month with Kenneth and me in Bend decades ago. When I was living in Colton, California, remember, across town from my mother, Beady lived in a town just a few miles away. She visited me in every house I lived in through the years—Oregon, Utah, and Arizona. Later on, she moved to Colorado and, of course, I went to Colorado to visit her. She spent a lot of time at the Williams cabin in the winter. She loved the snow. She loved Glyn and said he reminded her of a big Teddy bear.

She had married during WWII and had a son by that

husband. That marriage didn't last. She was single for quite a while. Then she married Chuck Martin. She had two children, Chickie and Dottie. I had Tim, so our children grew up together. We used to talk about things like who would get married first, who would have the first baby and we wondered what kind of mothers-in-law we would make. As we grew older, we would wonder which of us would die first. She beat me out on all counts—marriage, child and death.

When we were living in Havasu, Chuck was 58 years old. They were having a picnic on the beach down by the lake. Chuck had been out on a water ski and came in and sat down to have a beer. Soon he said he needed to start a fire if they were going to grill out. He stood up and dropped dead. The doctors said he was gone when he hit the ground. Beady lived 36 years longer. She never dated or married again. In 2014, I received a phone call from Dottie saying her mother had passed. I knew she was in poor health, and I will never forgive myself for not going to see her before she passed.

I have known a lot of friends in my life, but I had few true friends. Beady, Ellie, Pat, Cowboy Bob and Shirley Bullock, Jerry and Marie Smith, Steve and Bonnie James, and my daughter-in-law, Betz, were my true, true friends. I have added new true friends to that list, which I will cover later.

Our Golden Girls

Then there are my "golden girls." There are only two left.

In the beginning there were four of them, including Aunt Eunice (Glyn's dad's sister), who lived to be 99 years old. When she was in her 80's, she had a little band with three people. She played the fiddle, one played a guitar and one played the mandolin. They would go around to the local nursing homes and senior living centers and play during the lunch hour. The other three members were Glyn's mom (Rowena) and two of his cousins, Wanda, and Maxine, aka Max.

The cousins are the only ones left. Wanda turned 90 in January of 2017. She has now been moved into a nursing home with full care, and it is difficult to have a conversation with her due to the dementia that has taken over her mind. Max was 93 on November 18, 2016, and has been in senior living for nine years. She's in good health but has a little trouble walking. She has an amazing memory and has always had one hell of a sense of humor. It didn't matter where we lived—California, Arizona, Utah, and Oregon—they always came to visit. They would usually spend a week. All we did when they were with us was laugh, eat and play games. I grew to love the gals so much. It is so sad that they are all too old to travel any more. I still go down to Tim and Betz's and spend the holidays with the family. And I always go see my golden girls.

Wanda and Max always did a lot of traveling, seeing the fall colors of New England, Washington DC, the Grand Ole Opry, and two trips to Hawaii, to name a few. On the New England trip, they flew into New York and stayed the night in a motel. The next morning they boarded the bus for the tour. It was full of people from England. Max thought the English people would be boring with no sense of humor. She told Wanda it was going to be a very dull trip. They traveled all day without any conversation.

That evening they stopped at a hotel for the night. The hostess stood in the front of the bus and announced, "If any of you people have any problems during the night, please don't hesitate to knock on my door, I'm here for you. I will be in room 6." Max stood up in the middle of the bus, put her hands on her hips and in a very low sexy voice, said, "If any of you gentlemen have a problem, I'll be in room 5," and the bus cracked up! The trip was enjoyed by all. A couple of years later, two of the women came from England to California to visit Max and Wanda. Max thought it was interesting that they were so surprised that there were free refills on coffee. Free! They went to a Mexican restaurant and the English said, "These people are from Mexico. Why are they living in the United States?" The ladies were of the old school, you're born in England and you die in England.

I used to say my cup runneth over. Glyn and I were so happy together. I had Tim and Betz and the grandkids. We were a happy family. Glyn and I had the best of two worlds. We had always been very active and blessed with mostly good health, except the heart troubles, and they were behind us.

My Back Pain

In 2000, I started to have back pain. I went to three doctors and received three different opinions. The pain was getting worse. We found that there was a new Mayo clinic in Phoenix. We went and found out I had a cyst on my spine and it was pressing on a nerve. I had the surgery and it relieved my pain. The doctor said he had to remove some bone to get to the nerve. I asked if that would be a problem and he said no. Wasn't long after my surgery that my pain was back. Another round of doctors. The last doctor recommended I go to Phoenix to a Dr. Jack Mayfield. I had to wait four weeks for an appointment. While I was waiting, I decided to buy new living room furniture. I put an ad in the paper and, as luck would have it, it was an old friend, Larry, the chiropractor I had gone to for years. I told him I needed help with my back, but after surgery they told me no more chiropractors.

He bought the furniture and said, "Give the medical boys a chance, and if they don't fix it, come see me." At this point, Glyn was lifting me in and out of bed, off and on the toilet. I decided to go see Larry and the first thing he did was x-ray my back. He came in the room and put the x-ray up and said, "See these little tabs on both sides of the spine? Those are what give your back stability. Your doctor cut away two of these tabs. You have very little stability in your back." When I saw Dr. Mayfield he agreed with Larry, and I needed metal in my back to replace the tabs. I had the surgery, and my back was fine.

While I was going through all of this I received a letter from Betz and this is what it said:

"Dear Nancy,

I know you're getting discouraged from your physical condition and it is getting you down. You have always been an encouragement to grandpa (Glyn), now it is time to do it for yourself. Maybe I can help you with a little influence from myself. I would like to tell you the many ways you have positively influenced me. Hopefully, I will help provide a more positive attitude that helps you.

Thank you for your vitality and enthusiasm for going and doing things. You forged forward with wonderful ideas. I always wonder where and how you do it. Even now when you're down your spirit stays uplifted. You have never let things get you down. Your projects on new decorating and wanting to stay current with your choice of clothing are so worth noticing.

Thank you for your inspiration in household affairs. I was never very interested in cooking or cleaning but your help and example has really helped me. You are my MOM when I live too far away from my own MOM to help.

Thank you for marrying grandpa. He has been your soulmate but also Tim's hunting and fishing buddy and all of our friends. His good nature and humor lightens our visit and times with you. He is one big teddy bear that I love and hold dear.

Thank you for providing my family with wonderful holidays and family get-togethers. I look back on family times and you and grandpa are always there. You are baking and providing fun times for us all. I hope I will be able to provide as wonderful times for my grandchildren as you have for yours. I remember the hunting times and the kids at Beaver when the kids played in the creek and we went on camping and picnicking trips that we all took together. You have exposed my children to the beauty and fun of nature because of the choices of homes you and papa (Glyn) have had.

Now time is passing and changes continue, may you know I am always thinking of you and pray that I will help you whenever I am needed as you have helped me. God has provided me a precious gift…you. Love, Betz."

Visiting Grandma's Grave

I said in the beginning of the book, the first ten years of my life I was raised by my mother and grandmother. I loved my grandmother so much and I thought of her often. One day Glyn and I were talking about her and I said how sorry I was that I had not been able to go to her funeral. I said I would like to go see her grave sometime. Glyn said, "Let's go." We left for Arkansas two days later. Glyn had been born in Texas, so we stopped at the town where he had been born on our way. We arrived at Hot Springs, Arkansas the next day. I started calling mortuaries and the first one said they had not buried an Ella Runyon. So I called the second one and she said the same. She said call the other one back because they don't know what they are doing half the time. I called back and yes, they had buried Ella Runyon. It was not in the town of Hot Springs, but in another town 15 miles away. This was odd to me because my grandmother had lived in Hot Springs all her life. Why would she go to another town to be buried? I don't remember the name of the town but we went there. In the South, there is a church on every corner. We drove past a church and with a car parked in front. I told Glyn they would know where the cemetery was. There was an older gentleman cleaning the church with his grandson. I asked him where the cemetery was located. He told me and said, "If you go past a bridge, you've gone too far." He said to his grandson, "Let's go, let's help this woman find her grandmother's grave."

    We went in the cemetery and there were no headstones around that we could see. I told Glyn, "If my mother didn't put a headstone on grandma's grave I will never forgive her." At one end of each grave there was a white rock, and this was the only markers. The old gentleman and Glyn started walking among the graves in hopes of finding something. Glyn was on the other side of the cemetery and yelled out, "I found her." There was a big, beautiful headstone. This was the answer to why my grandma wasn't buried in Hot Springs. It read, "Robert Burton Runyon; Ella West Runyon." They were buried side by side. Next to the grave there was a child's grave. Then I remembered my mom had told me she had a baby brother that had died as a child. Standing there at my grandma's grave, I realized how much I loved Glyn for bringing me there.

Glyn's Mother Dies

Two months after our trip to Arkansas Glyn's mother, Rowena, passed away. About a year before, Glyn's ex-wife and Pam, his oldest child, came over to Rowena's house and tried to talk her into making a will. It made her so mad after the way they had treated her. She called Glyn and said to come over so she could make out a will. She made out a living trust and left everything to Glyn. There wasn't a large amount of money left. She told Glyn, "I would like for you to give something to the grandkids; after all they are part of my family. Don't give Mitch any money, as he has owed me $11,000 for a long time with no effort to pay me."

We went over to San Luis Obispo and Glyn gave Pam and Jane each $10,000. He handed the paper Mitch had made up when he got the money from his grandmother. Glyn marked it PIF (paid in full). As you have already guessed, that went over like a fart in church.

One of many camping trips with grandchildren – Dana, Anne and Lynn

Anne, Dana and Lynn

Left to right – Lynn, Anne with Kadin, and Dana with Matthew

Log cabin in Williams, Arizona

Our last move – remodeling in La Pine, Oregon

First winter in La Pine, Oregon

This is the van we drove to Alaska. It's true – the mosquito should be their state bird.

Retirement and relaxing in La Pine

Glyn's first year in La Pine

We loved to go fishing.

With Kadin, our first great-grandchild

Glyn and our boat at Havasu, Arizona

Selling the Cabin In Williams, AZ

Another big change in our lives happened in 2003. We were spending the summer at the cabin in Williams. Glyn was complaining about being tired all the time and just didn't feel good. He was short of breath when he did work around the cabin. We made an appointment with the cardiologist in Flagstaff. After all the tests, the doctor said he would be fine but he would just need to live below a 5,000 foot elevation. "The air is just too thin up here for you." The cabin in Williams was at 6,800 feet elevation.

We packed up and went back to Havasu and soon Glyn felt fine. The thought of giving up the cabin was so sad. We both agreed it had to be. Also, the thought of living in Havasu year around didn't sound too good either. Here we are again, needing to move.

Coming Back to Central Oregon

We had always loved living in the woods, and hunting and fishing. We decided to choose the mountains at a lower elevation. I told him about Bend, Oregon, since it was only 3,600 feet elevation. It had a lot of hunting and fishing and was beautiful country. This all sounded good to him, and he was willing to take a look. At this point in time, Glyn was 78 and I was 76. We realized boating was going to be a thing of the past. It would be bank fishing from here on out.

I had not been back to Bend since the 1940's and now it was 2003. What a surprise! The city had really changed.

Remember, I cooked on a wood stove, had wood heat, and lived on an unpaved street (Northeast Franklin), which most of them were. We knew right away Bend was too big of a town for us! We had talked to one of Glyn's cousins before we left for Oregon. She said Harold and Jody Hargas, old friends to the Watts family, now lived in La Pine, Oregon. Glyn had gone to high school with Harold. We contacted Harold and Jody and they invited us over for dinner. We became close friends. We went to the John L. Scott real estate office in La Pine and started our search. Our real estate lady was Shirley Ingersoll. We became good friends and are still good friends to this day.

One of the first places Shirley showed us was in a little community called Wild River. The house was 1,400 square feet on the Deschutes River. We loved the location and the neighborhood was really nice. The view of the river was great. We looked at several other places, and I did what I had done when we were looking for land for the cabin in Williams. I called Tim and asked for his opinion. So he and Betz flew up. Now I have to tell a story about Tim.

While they were building the cabin in Utah, we went deer hunting in our RV. Tim didn't own his plane yet, so he flew commercial. Beady and her husband Chuck were coming from California to go hunting with us. Since they drove their RV and came through St. George, they picked up Tim at the airport. Tim slept on the couch in our RV. Glyn was a champion snorer, and he would hold his breath. With Tim sleeping so close, when Glyn would hold his breath, Tim would say to himself, "Breathe Glyn. Breathe Glyn. goddammit, Breathe Glyn." Glyn would take a breath and do it all over again. After the hunt was over and we were saying our goodbyes, someone asked Tim if he would fly up again next year. Tim said, "No, I will never sleep in the same room with Glyn Watts ever again!"

When the kids flew to La Pine, it was during deer season. The only motel we could get was at the Best Western, and it was a suite. When we told Tim and Betz we could only get one room, right away Tim was looking for a way out. He told Betz he didn't want to hurt our feelings but he really didn't want to sleep in the same room with Glyn. "I think we'll have to drive in to Bend." When Tim brought our luggage up to the room, he was relieved to see there was a bedroom, living room and kitchen. They slept in the bedroom with the door closed and Glyn and I slept on the couch.

The next morning Shirley took us around to look at several properties. I didn't take them to see the house on the river, as I had written it off as too small. The kids didn't like any of the properties and they went home without us having any prospects. Glyn and I stayed a few days and didn't find anything. We visited with the Hargas' and went home with no prospects. We really liked La Pine, because it was a really small town, which is what we wanted. The country was beautiful with Ponderosa Pines. There were eleven lakes in the area and the Big and Little Deschutes River. We decided on La Pine, even though the winters were cold and the summers cool. We figured at our age we would be cutting back on outdoor activities.

After Thanksgiving, we took the train back to La Pine, got a motel and called Shirley. We knew there was a lot on the other side of the river for sale. And Tim had found another lot for $35,000 on the internet on the west side of the river for sale. We told Shirley we just wanted to look at three properties. There was about eight inches of snow on the ground. We started with the lot on the east side of the river and walked a very long way and never did see the river. So we gave up on that one. The one Tim found on the internet was on the west side of the river. Shirley said, "You don't want that lot, because your back yard is right on Burgess Road, the main road to all the lakes."

Buying the Little Gray House

The only one left was the little gray house. It was small but it had good bones. Shirley made arrangements with a contractor and we met at the house. We told him what we wanted. It had three bedrooms and two baths. We wanted to take out one of the bedrooms and expand the living room and add a new master bedroom and bath. We also wanted to remove all the carpet and install wood floors and a new fireplace. The contractor said they could do it, so we bought the house. We visited with Harold and Jody and then left for Arizona. We signed the escrow papers by mail in January of 2004 and didn't come back to La Pine until April. Again, the condo and cabin went on the market as the ones before them. The contractor drew up the plans and sent them to us and we approved. They would start remodeling in April. This would give us a lot of time to pack and get ready for the move.

We brought things down from the cabin and had a huge garage sale at the condo in Havasu. One day during the sale a man asked, "Are you moving?" I said yes. He asked where we were moving and I told him Oregon. The man on the other side of the table asked where in Oregon and I said La Pine, a community called Wild River. He said he lived in Wild River. I told him we had bought a house and it turned out they were my new next door neighbors! What are the odds?

Glyn did a great job packing. The condo sold and we closed escrow at the same time we were moving to La Pine. The cabin took a little longer, but we still managed to sell before the bottom fell out of the real estate market. We hired a moving van and arrived at our new driveway 15 minutes after the van and we hadn't traveled with the van!

Finally, Home on the River

We lived in the new house for two weeks. When they started construction, we rented a single-wide mobile in Riverview Trailer Park for three months. Meanwhile, we bought all the furniture for the house. The furniture store stored everything for us and the day the house was finished we had all the furniture delivered. It took days to unpack all the boxes we had packed. There was a waterfall close and the rapids on the river. You could hear the river if you left your door open. The sound of the river came right into the house. All our company always slept with the windows open so they could hear it. We were in the middle of the forest and it was so beautiful.

When winter came, we settled in. I hadn't knitted in several years, so I decided to knit a sweater. We had never spent much time reading, as the winters in Havasu were mild. With TV, knitting, playing cards and reading, we kept busy. There is nothing more beautiful than falling snow and the trees covered in snow. Glyn was still able to shovel snow off the deck and carry in wood. We were content. We found out that a little nap once in a while was nice.

For the first couple of winters we drove down to Tim and Betz's house to share the holidays with the family. We stayed for a couple of months, as that really broke up the winter. When Glyn turned 80, he could no longer make the long drive and we started taking the train. We really enjoyed the train trips, and the holidays with the family were wonderful. I know you haven't been keeping track of all the homes Glyn and I had through the years, but there were eight. Someone once asked me which one did you like the best, and I said I loved them all equally.

A Lifetime of Remodeling

When we first married, we remodeled the Foster's Freeze and the house Glyn had just bought before we were married. That was just the beginning, we never stopped. We owned three mobile homes and added on screened-in porches, Arizona rooms, new carpet, paint and landscaping. We built two log cabins. To the one in Utah, we later added a big bay window and a bathroom upstairs. To the one in Williams we added decks, banisters and lots of landscaping. If the home was in the desert I decorated southwest style. If it was in the mountains, I decorated western and mountain. The last house was the La Pine home. We replaced the linoleum in the kitchen with hardwood floors and replaced the Formica counters with granite and all new appliances. We also added an extra 12 feet to the width of the garage. One day, Betz came to me and asked if they could add on to our house, because when we all got together there were 13 of us and it was really crowded. She and Tim wanted to pay for it. I said there are a couple of things we have to talk about first: 1) I don't have to clean it, and 2) I don't have to heat it in the winter.

They agreed, and said that will be taken care of. They added 1,200 square feet to our house: a family room 22 feet wide and 40 feet long. They added another upstairs bedroom and bath. We now have four bedrooms and four baths. The original 1,400 square foot little gray house had now become 3,200 square feet. They put in a fireplace and completely furnished the new addition.

New Friends in Wild River

The neighbors in Wild River were the nicest people you would ever want to meet. Almost all were senior citizens.

They continue to have parties and get-togethers and are lots of fun to be around. We lucked out with one neighbor, Steve and Bonnie James. I don't know if they adopted us or we adopted them. There are two kinds of people in this old world, one group says "what can I do you out of" and the other says "what can I do for you." Steve belongs in the latter. He is always doing something for someone and is one of the kindest people I have ever known. I am sure all the neighbors would agree.

Glyn Passes On

We have been in the house in Wild River for nine years and I'm sorry to say we're getting old. I am 85 and Glyn is 87. We have given up bank fishing, but still enjoy long drives in the forest. I am still in pretty good health but Glyn is failing. He has had a couple of stents put in his heart, a couple of mini strokes, had a pacemaker put in, and he isn't very active anymore. His greatest joy is watching old Western movies on TV. I asked him one day, "Haven't you seen this movie?" He said, "Yes, but I like to see it again." I believe he has seen all John Wayne's movies at least three or four times. He has lost so much weight he is down to 150 lbs. He still has that twinkle in his eye and that wonderful sense of humor.

Betz came up and stayed with me for two weeks. We called in hospice. They came twice a week and took his vitals and showered him. He complained about the catheter being put in and said it was not right to lay in bed and pee, so he pulled it out. He complained about the diapers. "I'm not puttin' those on, no no." We ordered him a hospital bed and put it in the living room. I slept on the couch and we held hands until we fell asleep. He said, "I'm not gettin' in that bed." Of course, he got in the bed. But his biggest complaint was the railings we had to put on the bed. He begged me, "Please don't fence me in. I'll be a good boy, I won't get up." I said, "I don't trust you Grandpa."

Glyn's Lasting Sense of Humor

Finally came time for the family to come and say their goodbyes. Anne, Jerod, Kadin and Skylar came first. Dana, Pete, Mathew and Kara came next. One night while Dana and Pete were here I had fed him his dinner and he said, "I'm going to sleep now." I told him, "We are going in the family room and play poker." He had a walker with a bicycle horn on it. I told him if you need anything, honk your horn. We were in the family room and here came grandpa with his walker. All he had on was his t-shirt and diaper. He strutted around the room like a fashion model and said, "This is my new wardrobe." Everyone was cracking up!

Tim came up alone. Glyn asked Tim if he would do a favor for him. Tim said, "You name it." Glyn asked for Tim to take him to dinner and to gamble. So Steve and Bonnie joined Tim, Glyn and me for dinner at a restaurant in Sunriver. When we came in the door, he told Steve he had to go to the bathroom. So they went down the hall and the bathrooms were on the right and the slot machines were on the left. He started to pull Steve to the left. Steve was surprised at his strength. He played the slots for a little while and won $231. On the way out the door he said, "I'm going out a winner!"

Betz and all the family left for home. The first night I was alone with Glyn I called and had someone from Visiting Angels come in. He came at 10:00 p.m. and stayed until 8:00 a.m. I had him sleep on the couch next to the hospital bed. It had been a long time since I had slept in my own bed and it sure felt good. He came for three nights in a row. When he came on the third night, Glyn had already passed. On February 28th, the Hospice nurse said, "He is in transition. He doesn't hear us or know anything." What a coincidence. I met him on February 28th, and although his body didn't pass until 10:00 p.m. on March 1st, his soul left on February 28th, 2013, ending 42 years of our togetherness.

The coroner came and took him away. The nurse from Hospice had come at 6:00 p.m. that evening to be with me when Glyn passed. She gathered up her things and left. At this point I'm sitting in the house all alone. I called Tim and Betz and said he was gone. I sat in this chair for a long time and, when I looked at my watch, it was 2:00 a.m. I thought I hadn't had dinner, so I got up and fixed myself something to eat. I don't even know what I fixed, my mind was blank. I went to bed. The next morning I came in the living room and there was the empty hospital bed. I called

Hospice and told them to come right away and take this damn bed. I can't stand to look at it any more. And they did.

I look back now and I don't know how I did that, alone without him. I kept telling myself it was his time. He had a good life, a long life. It was his time and I felt I would be with him soon. But that didn't happen. I do not need to go into how lonely it was. You have probably already figured that out. They say time heals and it does, to a point.

Glyn's Ashes

We planned on the family getting together on the 4th of July to take care of Glyn's ashes. I had asked Glyn what he wanted me to do with his ashes and he said, "Just take me down to the bridge and throw me in the water." Since we had spent so many hours on the water, it sounded like a good idea. But the river was all rapids, so we had a hard time finding a spot to have a little ceremony to sprinkle his ashes. I had not planned on buying an urn, but the mortician told me they have an urn that you put in the water and, in 10 to 15 minutes, it dissolves and the ashes float away in the water.

Betz and I had picked up the ashes and when we were all gathered on the 4th, Steve and Bonnie joined the family. We walked the river and found a little bypass on the river where the water was moving but quiet. Sue, the spiritual advisor from Hospice, agreed to come and say a few words. We gathered on the river, and Tim put the urn in the water. After Sue had spoken, Tim spoke. He said "Glyn and I always had a lot in common. We both loved to build things, we both loved to fish and hunt, and he always took such good care of my mom." I don't remember what else he said. I had bought a dozen red roses and gave everyone a rose. They walked over to the river and put the rose in the water as the ashes floated by. There was not a dry eye to be had. We walked back to the house and had arranged for a celebration of life. The neighbors came and we had a good time.

Remodeling after Grandpa Passed

I'm still living in the same house now for three years since he's been gone and I keep busy working in the yard and visiting with friends. I still go south to spend holidays with the family. It breaks up the long cold winter here in La Pine.

More Remodeling!

I started remodeling again; I guess it's in my blood. I put beams in the cathedral ceilings in the living room, rocks around the counter in the kitchen, tiled the floor in the guest bathroom and put shingles on the house siding. I decided to tear out part of the lawn and put in a stone patio, added a swing, chairs and fire pit. Since my home is halfway to the mailboxes for so many of my neighbors, they stop by on their way and visit. One day, another one of my neighbors came by on his bicycle and wheeled in. There were five people sitting on the patio. He said, "Nancy, you just pull 'em in off the street." I told him, "You have heard the story, 'you build it and they will come.' I built it and they came."

CHAPTER EIGHT

Losing Tim 2015

I started writing my story on January 7, 2015. Today is July 15, 2015. The last I wrote in this story was February 18, 2015, my 87th birthday. I put down my pen and went to bed. The next morning I got up at my usual time, turned on Fox News, fed the cats and fixed my breakfast. I did the dishes and the phone rang. It was my daughter-in-law, Betz Brown. She told me she had some very sad news and that I should turn off the TV and sit down. I right away thought something had happened to one of my grand- or great-grandchildren. I said, "OK, Betz, I'm sitting down." She said, "I don't know how to say this but Tim is dead."

The night before, he had told Betz that he would not be home for dinner. He said he had meetings all day in Fresno. After the meetings, he and his friends were going out for dinner. He had his day planned. When he did not get up the next morning, Betz went to wake him and he was lying face down on the bed. That had to have been the worst thing that had ever happened to Betz; I don't know how she was able to handle it. She is my dearest friend and always has been since the day they married. After she called me with the news, my granddaughter Annie got on the phone and told me she had called my best neighbors, Steve and Bonnie, and would stay on the phone with me until they got here to my house.

That night, I was on a shuttle on my way to the train heading to my son's home. I was sitting right behind the driver and had the seat to myself. I couldn't stop crying, but I was crying as softly as I could. When we made our first stop, the lady sitting behind me came and sat next to me, took my hand and said, "You're not alone, I am here for you." This stranger in the night came and sat with me and comforted me. There are a lot of wonderful people in this world. You will never know the comfort she gave me. I never knew her name, she didn't say, and I was so upset it didn't even occur to me.

I arrived in California the next afternoon. The grandkids picked me up at the station. When we got to Tim's house, I threw myself on the bed where he had died and cried my heart out. I stayed there for three weeks and it was so sad I had to go home. I went back to Tim's house two weeks later to take care of the ashes. When Betz and I went to pick up the ashes, the urn she had ordered had not come in. I said, "That's good Betz. Let's separate the ashes and take half to the ranch and half to Mt. Nutt." I'm getting ahead of my story but I have to continue. Kenneth, Tim and I had moved to the little ranch in Arizona when Tim was nine years old. He loved this place so very, very much. The other half of the ashes would go to Mt. Nutt.

The Mt. Nutt Story

Mt. Nutt is the tallest mountain in the Black Mountain range in Arizona. Tim was always fascinated by this mountain. When he was 13 or 14 years old, he would always say, "I am going to climb Mt. Nutt," and of course I told him, "I forbid it." One day, he and his friend Chuckie were out in the desert playing. He came home and said, "Mom, I have to get my .22 and you need to come with me. I want to show you something." We got in our old WWII jeep and drove up to a little knoll. He said, "Here mom, take my .22, look thru the scope and look at the top of Mt. Nutt." There, waving in the breeze, was a little white T-shirt. I looked at him and said, "You still have your T-shirt on." He said, "Chuckie's had a hole in his, so we left his!" As he got older, he started saying, "I want my ashes spread across the top of Mt. Nutt overlooking the ridge." We all knew that was his wish.

Taking Tim's Ashes to Mt. Nutt

All the family—Betz, my three granddaughters, Dana, Annie and Lynn, with their husbands and the four great-grandchildren: Kadin 9, Matthew 7, Skylar 5, and Kara 3—went to the ranch in Arizona. I hadn't been to the ranch for a long time, but I had kept in touch with Lois, the current owner of the ranch. She had lived on the ranch for 36 years. It was a sad and happy time to see Lois again. I never thought I would ever be on the ranch or see it again. It was good to come home. Lois, her husband Bill, Kenneth, Tim and I had a special love for the place that no others after us could understand.

(A note about Lois: As of Valentine's Day this year (2017), Lois has been on the ranch 39 years. She has improved and added on to the ranch house, and has always kept up on repairs everywhere on the ranch.)

The next day Lynn, Dana and her husband Pete, Annie and her husband Jerod, and the two oldest grandchildren, Kadin and Matthew, took the rest of the ashes and hiked to the base of Mt. Nutt. They were unable to climb the mountain, so they left one of his white T-shirts and his ashes at the base of the mountain. Leaving him so close to the mountain and in the desert that he loved so much would have made him happy.

The previous September before he died, Tim flew himself over to Kingman to a high school reunion. While there, he rented a car and drove out to the ranch. Lois was so happy; they spent the entire afternoon together. Before he left, he stood in front of the picture window in the living room, Lois said, for the longest time. She didn't interrupt his thoughts. When he came home, he was telling Dana about his trip. Dana asked, "When Lois dies, are you still going to buy the ranch?" He said, "Yes, I am." Dana asked about Lois' health, and Tim said, "She's in perfect health and she'll probably outlive me!" He had always planned to live his remaining years at the ranch. Sadly, that was not to be. However, when we spread half of his ashes on the ranch, we placed them at the foot of a hedgehog cactus that was in full bloom and in full view from the picture window.

Celebration of Life for Tim

While I was staying at Tim and Betz's home after his passing, one of the companies Tim worked for gave a celebration of life luncheon for Tim at a very nice restaurant. Many people came. A lot of people came up to me to tell me their story about Tim. A little Mexican man told me the story of how Tim helped him to become a citizen. Then he said Tim wrote a letter to Mexico and got his wife to come to America to live with him. He said I will never forget Tim Brown.

Another employee told her story. She was divorced and had three children and was pregnant. Her mother was home taking care of the children when she started labor while she was at work. She had no one to be with her while she was at the hospital. Tim said, "Come on Sylvia (the pregnant woman), let's go to the hospital." She was Tim's secretary. Tim stayed with her until the baby was born.

Another story I heard was from a man who said a lot of people complained that Tim was hard to work for, but he disagreed. With Tim, you did it right the first time, you did it now, and no excuses. My son was a good man, a caring man, and I will carry him in my heart until my death. When I came home from Arizona, I went through all the phases of grief. I was mad at Tim for not retiring and going fishing, as all people his age did. He was 67 years old and could well afford to retire. Everyone convinced me he was happy doing what he was doing. He really was doing everything right, health-wise. The pathologist and coroner said this man should not be here. He had lost weight, was eating right, taking his medicine, exercising. The coroner and pathologist said in all their years they had never seen a 67 year old man come in with a six-pack abdomen. He was in perfect physical condition.

He was a workaholic. He was working for two companies and had his own consulting business. Most of my grieving was for the things that Tim would never do or see again. I was so sad to think he would never ski down a slope again or catch a fish or see a sun rise or set, he would never see the forest or a rainy day. Then one day my phone rang and it was my old friend of 45 years, Cowboy Bob. I told Bob just what I had written about what Tim would never see again. And Bob said, "I don't know where you're coming from Nancy." I said, "What do you mean?" Bob said, "Tim did all those things. How many people own their own plane? He could fly anywhere he wanted to go. You have a beautiful elk above your fireplace. Tim shot that elk. He did it all. As a matter of fact, I wouldn't mind living Tim's life. Tim did more in his 67 years than I have done in my 88." All I can say now is, thank you Bob.

It is time to end this sad time in my life. The grieving is still there. I will end it with the obituary Annie wrote about her dad. She said it all:

Tim's official Navy portrait

Timothy Lee Brown

Timothy Lee Brown, age 67, died Thursday, February 19th, 2015, when his life abruptly ended from a massive seizure while sleeping.

Born June 9, 1947, in Bend, Oregon, Tim actually spent his early life growing up with his mother, Nancy and father, Kenneth on an isolated ranch in the beautiful desert near Kingman, Arizona. There he attended a one-room *school house and learned the life of a hard day's work. After graduating from Kingman High School at the age of 16, Tim attended University of Arizona and majored in Chemistry. Shortly after graduating, he joined the Navy and became a pilot, flying A-4 jets. While stationed in Okinawa he met his wife, Betty, who was teaching on a base there. They came to live in Lemoore, CA, where Tim left the Navy to start a family and begin working in the agriculture business. Tim put his chemistry degree to work for such companies as McCarthy, Britz, Simplot, and Integrow. There he dealt with the packaging, producing, and selling of fertilizer and sulfur.*

Survivors include his wife, Betty Brown, three daughters: Dana Mullin of Huntington Beach, Anne Strong of Hanford, and Lynn Brown of San Marcos. His mother, Nancy Watts, lives in La Pine, Oregon. He unfortunately left 4 grandchildren: Kadin 10, Matthew 8, Skylar 6, and Kara, 5. It was these people that knew him intimately and could say without a doubt that he was passionate for his profession and thrived on problem solving and other challenges when managing companies.

His friends and family will miss him desperately and will forever remember him for his stubborn, perfectionist attitude and hardworking demeanor. However, they are peaceful, knowing that he has left a legacy in his industry, but was still able to find time and happiness in flying his plane, skiing, hunting, and fly fishing. His family has fond memories of him and they are proud to have called him their son, husband, father, and papa.

Tim gets his wings.

Tim is sworn into the Navy.

Top:
Nancy and Tim with Tim's plane.
Middle:
Betz holding Kadin, Tim holding Matthew, Skylar standing. Back row – left to right – Jerod, Annie's husband; Annie, Lynn, Dana holding Kara, Dana's husband Pete.
Bottom:
Resting after opening Christmas gifts.

Betz… "6 Months Later"

In August, *six months* after Tim's passing, Betz's house caught on fire. It was a tragic thing for her and Anne. Four fire trucks and 40 firemen came to that fire! The fireman in charge told everyone that it was an attic fire and that they were going to break through the roof to get to the fire, leaving the interior of the house flooded. So he said everyone should grab something and get out as much as possible before this happens. All the things that were important to Tim were saved.

Betz rented a house for a year. She is now back in her home. In February, "6 months later", one of her sisters, Leah Grotte, died. Betz went back to Minnesota before her sister passed so she got to see Leah before she died. It was another sad time for her. She was a little apprehensive about the coming August because "6 months later" was coming up.

CHAPTER NINE

Where I Stand Today

Current Time

It is now October 2016. Tim has been gone 18 months. It is a beautiful day and fall is in the air. The quaking aspen are bright yellow and some are losing their leaves. I only have a few more days to sit in my swing on the patio in my front yard. Winter is almost here. It is a lonely time because some of my neighbors are snowbirds and they fly south for the winter. I will go to Betz's house in California and spend the holidays with the family. I will come home the day after Christmas.

I have learned to enjoy the winters in the 12 years I have been here. I will go down again in March for a couple of weeks to visit with the family. Betz is still my dearest friend, and I am so proud of my granddaughters. They are so beautiful, inside and out. Two of them have good marriages, and that is saying a lot in this day and age. So many young people go into marriage with the attitude, "if I don't like it, I'll just get a divorce." My grandchildren still believe in having dinner together with their family and talking about each other's day. My little Lynny, as I said before, has not found her niche yet, but she will. And needless to say, my great-grandchildren are the smartest, most handsome and cutest of all grandchildren. But I'm not biased. I am so lucky to have them all in my life.

I was so fortunate to have found two wonderful men to share my life. I truly loved both, and I was loved in return. There were so many ups and downs in my marriage to Kenneth, but I loved him so much. Both men had such a wonderful sense of humor. I have had much laughter in my life. My marriage to Glyn was very easy. He never got upset and sailed through life with an easygoing attitude; he always kept me laughing. He was much more affectionate than Kenneth, and he was a lot more romantic. I am so glad they came into my life. If I had to do it over again, except for the death of my son, I wouldn't change a thing. Because all of my challenges, good and bad, made me who I am today.

I am so lucky to have my good neighbors; they take good care of me. And I know if I need anything, they are there for me.

Neighbors

To name a few: Steve and Bonnie James, Bill and Bev Miller, Patsy and Vaughn Pieschl, Neva and Lee Huff, Marge Wilcox, Chuck and Lori Koerner, Jan and Calvin Hoke, John and Andy Payne, Sandy and Sandy Ruiz, and Bob & Wendy. So many of my good friends have either passed on or moved away. Virgil and Peggy Alsonso moved; Katie Culler passed; John and Marilyn Butler moved; Cathy and Nick Reiche moved; Mark & Mary Jo Constans (Mark passed).

A New Friend

One day I was sitting in my swing alone, and along came this cute little gal who introduced herself as Tammy Koldyke. She and her husband had recently moved into Wild River on the east side. She sat with me on the swing and we talked for a couple of hours getting to know one another. We became very close friends and, since we were both from the South originally (she was from South Carolina), we had a lot in common, even though we are 35 years apart.

When I told her I was writing a book, she offered to help with it and came regularly to type while I dictated. We have had a lot of fun times together over the past year, especially when writing the book. There were times when I thought our mothers were identical twins (especially when we compared their discipline methods). She would come to my house, sit in one of my recliners, put a pillow behind her back, and the computer on her lap, and I would talk. This book probably wouldn't have been finished for a couple more years without her help. She also helped with the recent renovation of my kitchen and the Southwest touches that I always wanted.

Tammy's husband, Brian, became increasingly unhappy

Beady's brother Ernie and his wife Jimmy with Beady's sister Jerry and me

Beady and I made same pose in 1995, repeated from 1991.

My two remaining Golden Girls – Wanda (left) and Maxine (right).

Glyn with three of the Golden Girls – Aunt Eunice, Wanda and Maxine.

with his job at the medical clinic in town. So they sold their house. They bought a very nice 37-foot fifth-wheel and are moving away next month, headed to the Southwest to become "desert rats" for a while. I gave her my old Arizona license plate from our Bronco that says just that—"Desert Rat." She pinned it up in her fifth-wheel and plans on trying to find Hidden Valley Ranch when they drive through Arizona. I hope she makes it and gets a feel for the ranch she came to know from writing this book. We both have a deep love of the desert, another connection we share. It is going to leave a big void in my life when she moves away.

Final Thoughts

I am 89 years old and I have told you all the important things that have happened in my life, so many memories. If I told you of all the fun times and laughter I have had, the book would be much larger than *Gone with the Wind*. Hopefully, I will be able to take care of myself and continue living in my home for the remaining years I have on this earth, until my appointment with God.

EPILOGUE

I am Tammy Koldyke and I had the honor of transcribing most of this book while Nancy dictated. Originally just a friendly neighbor, I became intrigued when Nancy told me she was writing the story of her life. For an 88-year-old person that is quite an endeavor. While working through the process of getting her memories on paper, we spent many long hours together. It was during that time that I began to learn more about my new friend and neighbor in a deeper way than if we had never undertaken this challenge together. The delicious lunches that she fixed, the fun stories she told that never made it into the book because they were just too numerous, and the loud political arguments we had, brought us so much closer in the 18 months we spent together than if we had never done this at all. She even told me some secrets that I will take to my grave.

During this time we realized we share a mutual love for the beauty and serenity of the desert. So her stories about the ranch in Oatman struck a chord with me. After this book was written, I made a trip to Arizona to pay the ranch a visit. Upon meeting Lois for the first time, I felt like I had known her all my life. She gave me a tour of Nancy's old homestead, inside and outside. Before I left I told her I wanted some alone time to walk around the ranch. I wanted to connect with where I was and the stories that I had learned about Nancy, Kenneth and Tim. One of the fun things about that area is the abundance of burros that meander on and off the property. However, while I was there and Lois was showing me around, there were no burros in sight. We saw their droppings, but never any burros, and I was disappointed.

   Just before I left, Lois left me to walk around the ranch by myself. I ended up on top of the hill behind the house, which overlooks a small valley on the other side. I stood there feeling the dry desert breeze across my face and spoke to Tim out loud. I told him that even though I had never met him, I felt like I knew him, and that I was so happy to be even a minor part of this journey with his mother. Just then, a burro stepped out from behind some bushes down in the valley and brayed three times. Indeed, I can say with utmost faith, that Tim's contented spirit is present and palpable at Hidden Valley Ranch.

www.ingramcontent.com/pod-product-compliance
Lightning Source LLC
Chambersburg PA
CBHW062058290426
44110CB00022B/2636